What is

The
Next Horizon?

A Study of Unusual Happenings
on the Path of Your Life

By Katie Halliwell

First edition 2023

Published by
Saturday Night Press Publications
England

snppbooks@gmail.com
www.snppbooks.com

ISBN 978-1-908421-62-3

www.snppbooks.com

DEDICATION

I dedicate this book to you all ~
to all those in both worlds
whom I have met on my journey ~
and to all of you who join me now.
May your journey be as enjoyable as mine.

ACKNOWLEDGEMENTS

I would like to thank my loving family and friends who have helped me through my path of life.

And Robert and Georgina Brake who were my mentors during my research.

Credit must go to Stewart Alexander, his Home Circle and the Spirit Team for all they have done to encourage communication between our two worlds.

Also to Tom and Ann Harrison for their support on the original trilogy which eventually led to the production of this book.

And a thank you must go to Warren James who set-up the spirit recordings on-line.

CONTENTS

Introduction

I was enjoying a get-together with my family when Adrian leaned over to me and said, "I have something to tell you." His wife, Jackie who was listening in, verified this interesting tale about to be told by saying, "We were on holiday and Adrian had not been drinking."

Adrian continued, "I was having a meal with friends when I felt something touch my right shoulder. I instantly knew it was Jackie's mum and this powerful sensation was such a shock to me, I began to cry, it was a very intense feeling and I wasn't even thinking of Jackie's mum. I had to walk away to compose myself."

Jackie confirmed that he went as white as a sheet.

Why the shock? It was at least two years after Jackie's mum (whom Adrian loved so much) had died.

After that initial experience, Adrian found it hard to accept what he clearly felt on his shoulder and the only rational explanation he could come up with was that it must have been a trick of the mind.

"Are you sure?" was my reply because clearly what he had just told me had shocked him at the time and continued to do so.

"Yes." Adrian confirmed, "It must have been a trick of the mind, definitely a trick of the mind."

Or was it? I wondered and I asked myself a question.

Had Adrian experienced a connection with the 'Next Horizon'?

A friend of mine, Jane, told me that she was driving through Easingwold[1], when she saw two kids ahead of her pushing a wooden cart full of dead rabbits hung over the edge. What she witnessed was in a very clear but rather strange grey. As Jane drove slowly past them, (trying to find a parking place), she noticed that the style of their dress was of a different age, possibly 1940s/50s. But what struck her most was the fact that one of them was carrying a shot gun bent over his

---

1. A market town on the edge of the North Yorkshire Moors.

arm, (something most certainly not allowed by law at the time of the sighting). Jane then watched them in her review mirror as she slowly drove on wishing she could have stopped to talk to them.

After hearing this, I asked myself another question:

Had Jane experienced a time warp? – a possible crack in the 'Next Horizon'.

By now, you are probably wondering what this 'Next Horizon' is all about.

Well, to my way of thinking, the 'Next Horizon' is something our material eyes cannot yet see, along with something we are reluctant to talk about, and we need to find out more because it is part of our destiny. It is a state of consciousness; another dimension; a mystery that can puzzle us to a great extent, especially when we come across a 'Next Horizon' experience at some point in our physical lives.

I too had a spontaneous occurrence of seeing my mum nine days after she died in 1976, (details in Chapter 4) and I have often wondered how many other people will have had similar extraordinary experiences which are rarely spoken about because they fear that they might be ridiculed.

There are other strange but true happenings kept under wraps, for example:-

Precognitive dreams,

Strange feelings that something is about to happen,

Evidence of the so-called dead living in another dimension,

Astral travelling, (flying through the air when the body is asleep)

Seeing spontaneous spheres of light,

Flashes of clear colourful images appearing when in meditation or when drifting off to sleep,

The list can be endless.

Instead of staying embarrassingly quiet – like most of us do, why not bring it all out into the open – to gain knowledge of where we are going, why we are here, and in doing so, perhaps discover this state of consciousness that awaits us all.

As the 'Next Horizon' is something we haven't yet reached but will do so one day, there is a lot to learn and with the help of this book, you could find food for thought and perhaps even create your own discussion groups. Or you may just wish to enjoy the story of a deaf child experiencing the challenges she had to face in the 1950s onwards.

I was born deaf and had to have extensive speech therapy during my early years. Not being able to talk properly was caused by my inability to hear the correct pronunciations of certain words and letters. This was indeed, a problem at the time.

Although I had the support of a loving and caring family, I did struggle with my education before being transferred to a deaf and dumb school in 1957.

Being cut off in many ways from the noisy material world, the silence of my thoughts allowed me to look deep within. It was an opening into an unseen world prompting many questions into the enigma of life.

As I tell my life story, which will include the extraordinary experiences I have had, the 'facts, theories and anomalies' section at the end of each chapter will invite you to investigate spiritual studies of your own choice along with recommended books to read.

Or perhaps you might like to consider my own research and views which could offer new ventures for you to explore. Who knows, you might discover that missing piece in your jigsaw of life.

After all, we are all pupils on this great school called Earth, so why not join with me and others in sharing these bizarre experiences with extra confidence and gain a greater perception of such anomalies beyond the present understanding of science.

Chapter One

The Wrong School

It was winter, the snow had fallen and I found an icy patch on the tarmac of the school playground looking very much like a sheet of glass. It was fascinating, so much so, that I slid my foot along this smooth surface wondering what made it like that. Suddenly I was pushed violently away by one of the boys who had apparently made this icy slide for themselves. I had not noticed a queue of them at a distance waiting for their turn to run up to the slide in a competition to find out who could skim the furthest. I could see them all shouting and waving at me to move out of the way, but of course I could not hear them.

This was one of many incidents I experienced in the playground at Trinity School. I can't remember how old I would be at the time, but I reckon I must have been about 5 or 6 years. To prevent further incidents like this, I found it safer to keep out of the way by retreating to my favourite corner of the playground and watch the children play.

Often I was confused because I did not know what I had done wrong. Even inside the school I would find myself baffled, not knowing why certain things were happening, such as being made to stand facing the entire school congregation simply because I had not brought any fruit or vegetables for the school harvest festival. To this very day I remember standing there in total bewilderment wondering how everyone knew to bring a harvest gift but not me.

How was I to know at such a young age that my deafness was the cause of so many confusions and misunderstandings?

Being a deaf child at a normal hearing school in the 1950s was not like it is now and there was no such thing as teaching assistants to help deaf pupils keep pace with their education. Often I was left alone wondering what to do with myself.

Because deafness was a bit of a stigma in those days, certain individuals would often tease hearing-impaired children and in my case I was frequently tormented by the boys at this school who had no knowledge of hearing difficulties and no sense of empathy what-so-ever.

I could not talk properly and because of this impediment it was necessary for me to make regular visits to a speech therapist. Mum would take me to see Miss Foster, a kind and patient lady who did her utmost to help me pronounce not only words but letters of the alphabet correctly. (Years later, I asked Dad if he remembered how I used to talk and he told me that I would say things like 'Yoe' instead of 'Joe' and 'Didy dird' instead of 'Dicky bird').

This was taken about the time of Christine's story (below), with Mum and Dad sitting behind us.

Children were not the only people I had problems with. My sister Christine, who is eight years older, has her own story to tell:

"When Katie was about four or five years old we were taking the bus back from visiting Grandma Halliwell and sitting on the top deck at the front she was standing 'driving' the bus. She wanted to pay the bus conductor and when he came up she said where she wanted to go. Unfortunately, she couldn't say it properly and he just turned to me and asked me outright if she was "daft or what".

I was only twelve or thirteen but I was so mad I shouted at him that she was deaf and the look on her poor little face has stayed with me all my life – she was SO upset. He just went off and couldn't have cared less. I vowed then that no-one else would treat her like that if I was around."

The obvious cause of my speech deficiency was simply because I could not hear the words spoken by other people.

Grandma Halliwell was a loving and caring person who looked after me with fierce protection. I did not talk much in my very early years and like Mum and Dad, for the first few years, she did not realise I was deaf.

There was a very close bond between Grandma and her niece Bessie. The picture here of me and Auntie Bessie was taken in 2007.

She too, has her story to tell:

"Katie's Grandma (my Auntie Edith) would often visit my father Harold and mother Alberta Lavinia (known as Vina) in Doncaster. Back then I can remember my mother saying, "I think Katie is deaf," and Auntie Edith would not accept her suggestion. She said the reason for Katie not talking was because Christine never stopped chattering."

Unlike now, doctors and nurses did not realise how important it was to test a baby's hearing soon after birth and for some time – according to Christine – my parents thought I was backward. Christine told me that Mum once gave her a metal tray and asked her to drop it at the foot of the stairs after I had been taken up the flight of steps and into the bedroom. Christine did the honours and Mum was horrified to see no response or reaction from me as she heard the loud clash. It was then Mum realised that I was indeed deaf and she took the decision to take me to the doctor to check out my hearing.

My medical notes indicated that I had hearing loss, slight general backwardness and defective speech. It was recommended that the removal of my tonsils and adenoids could be of benefit. I had the operation, but there was no change in my hearing.

The next move saw me as a patient visiting a Professor in Manchester[1] who noticed that I did not like wearing a hearing aid. He suggested that I should receive help and training on the use of a new hearing aid at an Ear, Nose and Throat clinic where a qualified teacher of the deaf would be able to give instructions to my parents.

This new hearing aid was so much better and less cumbersome to wear. I don't remember much about my very first hearing aid, but Dad told me that it was a big box at my hip held by a strap over my opposite shoulder. This box (the battery) had a wire linking up to another box on my other hip (the hearing aid) which had a long lead up to my left ear. This type of contraption was more suited for an adult to wear around the neck and chest area, but would hang on a small child like two shoulder bags.

I am pleased to say that hearing aids have advanced tremendously now that we have behind the ear models.

In my later school days, I wore a smaller box hearing aid with a long lead up to my left ear and because this was quite noticeable, there were many times when I was called a deaf lug in my face and to avoid this embarrassment, I often felt the need to cover up the aid as much as possible.

Here is part of a photograph, which is the only reference I can find, showing the smaller box hearing aid slotted into my front right pocket.

This single box hearing aid has a long lead to my left ear.

During the 1950s, only one box hearing aid was provided for the worst ear, nowadays behind the ear models are supplied for both ears which is necessary for a more accurate audio balance.

---

1. A city in the North-West of England.

Grandma Halliwell did her utmost to help me whenever she could. She even suggested I wear ear-muffs to protect my ears – bless her.

One day when I visited Grandma Halliwell, I saw an ice cream van parked outside and wanted to go and buy a lolly on my own. As Grandma stood at the door watching, I asked for an orange lolly. The lady serving in the van hastily took my money and shoved a white lolly in my hand and quickly told the driver to set off. Obviously I could not pronounce the word orange correctly and ended up feeling quite upset at being left on the pavement with the wrong flavoured lolly. Grandma, understanding my dilemma then took me to the local shop to buy an orange one.

Grandma Halliwell

I was often bewildered by similar predicaments, and I don't remember anything good about Trinity School. I most certainly have not forgotten the isolation and the confusions I experienced there. One day Mum was asked to see the headmistress who was concerned about me not being able to write my own name. This indicated that my education was suffering and that something had to be done.

Mum of course was very upset. I didn't even know what the letter 'a' was and I remember Christine creating a game for me. She cut out pieces of paper, each containing a letter and mixed them up on a table and my task was to place the letters into the correct order to make up my name. Christine would spend a lot of time with me, giving me the support and education I desperately needed at that particular time.

Looking back, I can now appreciate the problem my parents were faced with because in the 1950s they had special schools for the deaf and dumb and the word 'dumb' understandably horrified them intensively. Because of this indignity, they genuinely thought that it would be better for me to be educated at our local school.

Mum talked about this problem with my speech therapist who recommended a highly esteemed school for the deaf. She advised Mum not to judge the school at face value simply as a 'deaf and dumb' institution, but to look into the expertise they had to offer in improving my speech and education. After much thought, my parents then reluctantly decided that it was time to pay a visit to this school.

As we approached the gates in the car, we all saw the sign in big letters, 'Odsal House School for the Deaf and Dumb'. Dad stopped the car to study this billboard and started talking to Mum. Being the quizzical little girl at the back, I wanted to know why we had stopped and what they were looking at. They told me that they were not happy about the wording on the school billboard and I looked at it asking what was wrong. It was then they explained to me the meaning of the word dumb and this is why I can clearly remember such details to this very day.

Thankfully it was not long before it was generally realised that deaf people are not dumb and the offending word was soon to be removed from the school's billboard.

We were given a tour of the school by the headmistress and I can vividly remember her testing me out on some of the school's special hearing equipment. I sat at a desk wearing headphones and the headmistress stood behind me as far as she could at the back of the room and talked into a microphone. I had the disadvantage of not being able to look at her, but I heard every word she said and my parents were quite impressed. It was decided there and then, that this was the school for me.

Facts, Theories and Anomalies relating to this Chapter

Subject – Possible Karma?

Mum had toxaemia when she was pregnant and I had to be prematurely induced at 8 months otherwise we would have both died. This forced birth was thought to have caused my deafness – a non development of some of the hairs in the cochlear. In the fifties it was known as nervous deafness and nothing could be surgically done to rectify it.

You may or may not agree with me, but I believe you choose your parents before you are born into this life (or state of consciousness) on Earth.

Was it my karma to be deaf, or did I choose to be so?

For readers who may not know much about Karma, I do believe that certain souls choose to reincarnate to right the wrongs made in their past lives. For example, if I have misunderstood the problems of, or mistreated, a deaf person in my past life, then could it be that I chose to come back to find out what it is like to be deaf?

Who knows?

Reincarnation is an interesting subject and some people believe that many souls do return for different reasons, be it for Karmic debt, love or teaching.

When I look back, I often wonder how my life would have been if I had been able to hear. Perhaps my deafness was a kind of advantage because it acted as a blockage to the noisy material world and therefore enabled me to become isolated in such a way that I could be at one with myself and the universe. Without my hearing aids I am able to experience total silence and this helps me to concentrate on the world of thought, often referred to as the 'Spirit World'.

This ability certainly led to me writing this book.

As this is the first point of 'facts, theories and anomalies', and this book is focused on unusual happenings and spirit communication as against reincarnation, I would suggest (for now) you might like to consider this page as food for thought before reading more of my story and about other phenomena at the end of each chapter.

Chapter Two

Such a Contrast

My first day at Odsal House School was quite daunting and with the school being 6½ miles (10½ km) away it seemed so terribly far from home. Although I did not like Trinity School, it was always comforting to know that my loving family lived within walking distance. The very thought of going on those long bus journeys to Odsal House upset me to such an extent I would often complain of tummy ache, in the hope that they would let me stay at home.

The Odsal House School accepted deaf children from neighbouring towns around the vicinity, and a lady was commissioned to escort a small group of us from our home town to the school. However, I would start to cry when I was put on the big double-decker bus because being so far away from home was a considerable worry for me.

On the plus side, it was a relief to discover that the girls had a separate playground and even though I knew the boys here could not torment me as they did at the previous school, I still looked for a favourite corner and found one to watch the children play. In a little while, a group of girls gathered together and beckoned me to join them. Truthfully, I actually found this to be somewhat unnerving and I did not quite know what to do. Soon, however, one of the girls took me under her wing and introduced me to the other girls and I was amazed to discover how easy it was to communicate with them. They would tap me on the shoulder to get my attention first and then speak slowly face to face enabling me to watch their lips and hear words with ease.

The classes were different too, much smaller in number and our desks were placed in a horseshoe position so that we pupils could see the teacher and each other. My visits to Miss Foster had come to an end because speech lessons were included in the school timetable. It was the headmistress's intention to teach us to talk correctly so that we would be able to cope in the hearing world. To ensure that we did learn to talk, sign language was strictly forbidden throughout school hours.

Odsal House was a huge contrast to the Trinity School in which where I was pushed away and often ignored as here at the new school I was invited to join in.

Although it took me a while to settle in, something good was happening; my confidence was growing as I developed a sense of belonging.

* * * * *

Having written about my experiences at the deaf school, I think now is the time to introduce my home and family.

Our small terrace house was situated in an industrial town on the verge of the Pennines, a chain of hills in the North West of England.

As a family, we were not religious, but did attend a congregational church mainly for the community aspect rather than the actual ecclesiastical services. Mum would occasionally go to communion and Christine and I attended the Sunday school classes, but my visits were short lived. Maybe it was because I could not hear well enough to get involved?

We were a small family as both my Mum and Dad had no siblings and Christine was, and is my only sister.

I never knew my grandfathers, they had passed to spirit before I was born, but both my grandmothers were still alive. My mother's mother was quite petite and we called her Little Grandma and Dad's mother being tall and slim was known as Big Grandma.

As you read this book, you may wonder why not much has been mentioned about Little Grandma. This is because her health started to deteriorate while I was at a young age, and as a result of a long illness she died in 1961.

I was very fortunate to be born into this caring and loving family and we regularly played board games which I thoroughly enjoyed. I also remember helping Dad make children's tricycles. Dad would collect scrap ones and then renovate them and it was my job to paint the spokes on the wheels, a delicate task, which promoted patience for my future artistic talent. As Christine trained to become a private secretary, she was also an amateur actress and would use her imaginative skills in various ways. We were once on holiday staying at a house with a beautiful garden, a far cry from the blackened stoned street where we lived. Enhanced by trees around the garden, Christine told me some beautiful stories about the fairies. She picked up an acorn and explained how they like to wear the cups as hats, so I gathered a few of them, painted them in different colours and left them outside for the fairies to collect. Later that day, I went back out to see if they had taken them – and to my delight they had - because there was a message written on a leaf saying "Thank you Katie."

Such was the closeness of our family love.

This happy family photograph of Dad, me, Christine and Mum was taken while we were away on another holiday.

Our neighbours were a very closely knit society and I can remember the names of nearly all of them to this very day. I would often run across the back street to visit Auntie Edna and Uncle Arnold. They were not related but it was customary in those days to address Mum and Dad's friends as Auntie and Uncle. I loved to play with Uncle Arnold, he would throw a ball to me with such a spin and if it touched the floor it would bounce straight back to him causing me to squeal with laughter. We would also take regular trips to the local park to kick a ball around. Then, one day, he became very ill and I was too young to understand the meaning of cancer. I don't actually remember anything about his passing, but for a time, I did wonder why he wasn't around anymore.

On Sundays, Christine and I would routinely visit Big Grandma for tea, and coming home one night, Christine pointed up to the sky and showed me how to find the North Star. She then directed my gaze to the Great Bear and other constellations. I was fascinated with all this and it brought about my interest in Astronomy.

My next Christmas present from Mum and Dad was to be a telescope and I would spend many hours surveying the craters on the moon and looking into the depths of space seeking out anything the naked eye could not see. It was then, I began to wonder where space ends – or does it end?

My main hobbies were art and long distance running. Art was to become my career and my track running found me travelling round the country, with Mum, Dad and Christine cheering me on. I was often a winner in the National Deaf Championships, particularly in the 440 and 880 yard races (now 400 and 800 metres).

I reckon the walks to Trinity school with Dad helped me to become a successful runner because he would step out at such a pace causing me to run to keep up with him. A teacher at Odsal House School became my mentor and coach, often visiting the Harriers[1] to watch me run. I would train whenever I could, making time to jog round the school playing fields at lunchtime and spending many an hour keeping fit on a running track nearby. As well as track running I became a cross country runner and found myself competing for not only two local towns, but the county of Yorkshire as well.

My ultimate event was representing Great Britain in the Deaf Olympics in Belgrade, Yugoslavia (now Serbia) in 1969. I didn't bring home any medals, but it was certainly an exciting experience to remember.

---

1. My local running club.

Facts, Theories and Anomalies relating to this Chapter

Subject – Spirit Communication and Psychic Art.

Here we have an extraordinary piece of evidential spirit communication.

I would like to fast forward to the year 1989.

My very first visit to a Spiritualist Church was at Huddersfield in the summer of 1989. I liked this church so much I eventually decided to become a member and attended most Sundays (As detailed in Chapter 5). After gaining confidence, and knowing a bit more about Spiritualism, I then started to visit other Spiritualist Churches and Sowerby Bridge was one of them.

Sunday 24th September 1989 saw me visiting the Sowerby Bridge Spiritualist church and I sat next to a lady who was a complete stranger until we got talking after we introduced ourselves. The lady was called Joan and after the service I offered her a lift home. She invited me in for coffee and when I walked into her room I saw some excellent psychic drawings on the wall. Joan told me the name of the psychic artist who lived in Sheffield and said if I was interested, I could write to him including a passport photograph of myself for him to meditate on.

On Thursday 28th September I wrote to the above psychic artist requesting an illustration of any spirit person who might be around me at the time. I was a total stranger to this psychic artist and he knew nothing about my past. I was not happy about sending a passport photograph because I did not want the artist to pick out any of my facial features giving him the opportunity to make the drawings look like family members. So I sent him this photograph below and as you can see, my face is small enough to minimize any possibility of fraudulent activity.

On Sunday 1st October, I continued with my weekly visits to the Huddersfield Spiritualist church and was given my very first message.

At this stage, I would like to point out that I was a very inquisitive person with the intention of testing the medium. I would refuse to answer any question he/she might ask because I did not want to disclose any hints, clues or even body language which could be used for a 'cold reading'.[1]

The visiting platform medium from Rotherham looked at me and said, "I'm coming to you first because since the service began, the spirit people have been eager to give you this message".

"Look at the photographs and you will see the picture."

The medium then gave me a quizzical look and asked, "Does that mean anything to you?"

My reply was, "No."

He hesitated and then said, "That message is very important and it will mean something to you later on. Now I must move on to somebody else."

It was a very short message indeed and I was not at all impressed.

In actual fact, I had lied to the medium because I wanted him to tell me why he was giving me that message and I fully expected the spirit people to inform him of its importance. Although I must admit, as soon as the medium relayed that message to me, I did think of those psychic drawings I had requested four days earlier. Hind-sight tells me that I should have mentioned this to him instead of just saying no.

Like many first timers in a Spiritualist church, my way of thinking (via the brain) expected impressive evidential proof from the medium. What I was not aware of at the time was a process of communication. I now know of it as 'thought energy', a fast transmission instantaneously induced by the mind. For example: Why did I think of my request for the psychic drawings when the medium said, "Look at the photographs and you will see the picture."? After recognising this possibility, I came to the conclusion that the brain is a mere instrument of the body which dies at death, but my individual personality and character, known to many as the 'thought energy' of the mind, live on.

To my way of thinking, this creative 'thought energy' inspires the brain with spiritual knowledge which cannot always be accepted

1. A cold reading is when the medium watches and plays on the audience's reactions, and picking a recipient makes them think he is communicating with spirit when he isn't.

because the data is not often logical. The brain, (being finite) can only take in limited facts while the 'mind' with its wider vista of knowledge is infinite.

Three days later on **Wednesday 4th October**, I received three pencil drawings through the post from the psychic artist in Sheffield. Glancing at them before I set off for work (expecting to see Mum or Grandma) caused me to reject the illustrations because I did not recognise any of the faces.

When I was driving to work, I suddenly remembered the message I had received the previous Sunday, "Look at the photographs and you will see the picture." Indeed my curiosity got the better of me and as soon as I got back home that evening, I rummaged through a box of old photographs.

The only drawing I could not really match up was (A). The nearest likeliness I could find was photograph 1. The gentleman in the drawing has a shorter chin and is not wearing spectacles. Some people thought it was the same person, but I was not convinced.

A   1

The other two drawings opposite, I was happy to accept. The drawing of the lady (B) bears some resemblance with photograph 2.

The two people in 'A' and 'B' are probably Big Grandma's brother Harold and his wife Vina, when you compare them with the photos.

B   2

The third drawing (C) bears a resemblance to Uncle Arnold (photograph 3).

C   3

This is the Uncle Arnold mentioned earlier in this chapter and I had completely forgotten what he looked like.

I had not recognised Uncle Harold and Auntie Vina when I glanced at the drawings, simply because I had not seen them for a great number of years and had forgotten what they looked like.

This short message –'*Look at the photographs and you will see the picture.*' – now began to impress me. The very fact that a total stranger, a medium from Rotherham, should connect the psychic drawings drawn by a man from Sheffield, to an unknown face in the audience in Huddersfield, brought it home to me that there is a lot more to spirit communication than meets the eye. Had I not got that message, I would not have looked at the photographs.

Let us analyse the events:-

Sunday 24th September – I met a lady at Sowerby Bridge Spiritualist Church who told me about a psychic artist in Sheffield.

Thursday 28th September – I wrote to the recommended psychic artist.

Sunday 1st October – I received a message from a visiting medium from Rotherham at Huddersfield Spiritualist Church 'Look at the photographs and you will see the picture' along with a statement that this message will mean something to me later on.

Wednesday morning 4th October – I received the psychic drawings and rejected them.

Wednesday evening 4th October - I decided to rummage through a box of old photographs and found three possible links to the illustrations.

Two different churches were involved, one in Sowerby Bridge and the other in Huddersfield and two different mediums, one from Sheffield and the other from Rotherham. Surely this connection on the one subject is no coincidence and I believe it was all planned by our spirit friends.

This breakthrough then prompted me to start making notes and record all forms of spirit communication whenever possible.

My keen and intensive research began.

------- 000 -------

Recommended book relating to this chapter

Displaying many pages of fascinating psychic portraits along with photographs for comparison, this book is a must read for those interested in psychic art.

'Faces of the Living Dead - The amazing psychic art of Frank Leah' by Paul Miller (ISBN 9780955705052).

(Further reading references relating to different methods of Spirit Communication will be mentioned in this book– so – please read on and find out more).

Chapter Three

Moving On

My loving family gave me a lot of moral support during the difficult years of my youth, and my confidence increased to the extent that I became a mischievous little imp enjoying the jokes I would purchase at the corner shop. Poor Christine bore the brunt of it all, like finding joke spiders and bugs in her bed while I pretended to be asleep waiting for a good laugh.

Talking of sleep, like most children, I did dream and occasionally I had some nightmares.

I once dreamt of Mum and Dad's bedroom being on fire and when I woke up, Mum had to calm me down convincing me that it was only a bad dream. Like most parents, Mum and Dad did have their arguments and looking back, I wonder if this dream was connected to something happening between them at the time?

One strange phenomenon I can remember happened outside on the street when I was a youngster. I was running towards the gas lamp where we children in the neighbourhood would meet and play. To my disappointment, nobody was there and as I slowly approached the gas lamp, out of the blue I heard a male voice from behind say, "Go and help your Mum wash up." The voice was loud and clear with an air of authority and I immediately shouted "No," before turning round to find nobody there. This certainly freaked me out and I began to wonder if God had been talking to me as I frantically continued to look around. In panic mode, I decided to go back to the house and when I got near to the entrance, I saw the door open and Mum popped her head out. As soon as she saw me, she said, "Oh, there you are Katie, come and help me wash up."

Was this some kind of telepathy?

The year 1963 saw Dad involved in a terrible car accident. He suffered broken ribs and a punctured lung, was hospitalised and had to spend a fair amount of time convalescing before he could return to work.

Christine married Michael in 1965 and Big Grandma moved into a nursing home allowing them to buy her house. Mum, Dad and I moved from our terrace home in October of that year to the semi-detached house I now reside in. Back then it was such a delight to move to the outskirts of the town where we had a garden, and it was such a pleasure to look out of the windows at a green field.

In the previous chapter I mentioned the black-stoned street of our abode and believe me; the stones were truly blackened by industrial smoke lingering in the valley. The locals would call this valley the 'devil's cauldron' because looking down at the town from the hills, only the tips of the tall mill chimneys could be seen poking out of the thick grey smog.

(As a matter of historical interest, because the mills were shut on Sundays, the air was cleaner on Mondays and this is why Mondays would always be wash days with laundry hung out to dry on nearly every street.)

In my childhood in the 50s and 60s, my home town was peppered with spinning mills billowing out grey/black smoke and I can remember sitting on the steps of our terrace house looking deeply into the black stained stone and seeing tiny pin prick sparkles of colour. I marvelled at these little specks of red, silver and gold etc. Even at that young age I had the ability to find hidden beauty in something so soiled, and to observe such tiny detail was second nature to me. Apparently, when I was just one year old, I would focus on anything small and pick it up between my finger and thumb – no wonder my artwork was always done in fine detail. Maybe it was because I was deaf, I would use my eyes to concentrate intensely on a particular object more than any normal person might do.

Eventually, the town became a smokeless zone, with the district being banned from burning coal. From then on, smokeless coal, referred to as coke, was the accepted heating fuel and everything was cleaned up.

Despite the smog and grime, there was loving community care among the neighbours on the street, which sadly is something that has declined in today's age of television and computers.

As for television, I did enjoy the action programmes, but could never follow the true meaning of the story because I struggled to hear the spoken word, (a hearing aid in those days would amplify sound but the clarity of words would still be muddled). Most of the time I concentrated on playing out, looking at the stars, painting pictures and training to be a long distance runner. I was never interested in fashion or pop music, but I found an attraction to classical music. Even though I am deaf and will never be able to hear music as it should be heard, the hearing aids did help me to enjoy what I was able to pick up. Whatever music I could hear encouraged me to drift into a harmonious bliss as I imagined beautiful scenes to the rhythm of sound.

Although I was quite successful at winning prizes in art and running, I left school without any qualifications apart from one 'O' level in Art which was gained from attending evening classes. Realising that art was my potential, Dad arranged for me to have an interview with the head designer at a large carpet manufacturer and it was on his recommendation that I attend a School of Art for two years.

Sadly this school was to bring back painful memories of Trinity. The confusions and misunderstandings unfortunately returned and I was often left out on the socialising side of student life allowing isolation to slowly creep back in again. However, concentrating on my art was a great escape and this helped me to build a strong portfolio which won me a place at a College of Art where I spent the next three years studying commercial art, display/exhibition work and typographic design.

Printing and typographic design became my main subject.

As for the spiritual side of my life, I continued to look for answers even down to studying every sentence of the Bible in the hope of finding some clues as to why we are here and where is heaven. I also spent many a peaceful hour studying and gazing upon the beauty of flowers appreciating their delicate and colourful petals especially during meditation.

What I didn't realise back then, was that in acknowledging such wonderful natural beauty, I was engaging in a thought condition which is most welcomed by the Spirit World.

Facts, Theories and Anomalies relating to this Chapter

Subject – Dreams.

A dream is real to us until we wake up. This is an interesting statement which brings about a further question. Is your life on Earth a learning state of consciousness which appears real at the time until after physical death when you wake up in the Spirit World – and does this mean that your life on Earth then will seem like a dream?

Is this why our spirit friends keep telling us that theirs is the real world – not ours?

Some people dream in colour, others in black and white, some say they don't dream at all. Whatever people say, dreams in my opinion are either the result of an over active brain, a recollection of something that has happened or seen, or perhaps it may be a spiritual dream which is often experienced in symbolic form.

I can always tell when I have had a spiritual dream because it leaves a lasting impression and keeping a dream diary has for me been beneficial.

I once dreamt that I was waiting in a queue at the till of a bookshop and as I looked around, I saw June Winchester's[1] head above the book shelves. She looked up and saw me, then motioned that she would like a word. Next moment I found myself sitting at a coffee table chatting to her and then I woke up.

After I got up that morning, I set off to go shopping and when I arrived back home there was an answer-phone message waiting for me. Strangely enough, it was June asking me to ring her. I rang back and her husband Alf answered my telephone call informing me that June was out, but he could tell me the message himself. A lady called Sylvia had passed away and it was her wish that I sell her spiritual books on our bookstall at the next seminar. Her friend Audrey had got these books at her home and she had asked June if she could contact me with a request to pick them up.

I was quite staggered and told Alf my dream – he was also amazed and then he cracked out laughing, confirming that whenever he happens to lose June in a small supermarket, he can often see her head above the shelves as she is quite a tall person.

This dream about the bookshop and June wanting to contact me

---

1. June and Alf Winchester organised seminars entitled, 'Stewart Alexander and Friends' and my usual job was to look after the bookstall.

really did relate to events that happened the very next day – and no doubt about it, it was precognitive.

While I was a student at the College of Art, I once dreamt that I was flying over the college itself and over the twisted lane leading to the annexe. This bird's eye view of the lane and roof tops was very clear indeed and I can only assume that I must have been astral travelling while my physical body was asleep. I can also remember vivid 'dreams' of flying out of my house through the front bedroom window and at the same time, dodging the telephone wires.

There is one dream I shall never forget (or was it a dream?) – an experience I encountered in the 1980s and that was when I woke up in the darkness of my bedroom and saw a silver face gliding towards me. At first, I thought it was the spirit of Big Grandma when she was a lot younger because her face actually looked like me. However, thinking about it, I wonder if I might have seen myself returning to my physical body, because I did wake up with a jerk?

Weird or what?

If you are interested in dreams, you could create a dream diary.

As for my personal experience on hearing the male voice on the street (as mentioned in the fourth paragraph on page 27), was it telepathy, my subconscious mind or a spirit person talking to me.

Who knows?

------- OOO -------

Keeping a Dream Diary

If you do remember your dreams, you might like to keep a dream diary.

You will need a note book and pen ready at the side of your bed so that as soon as you wake up, you can write down your details fresh from memory.

It is important to do this because less intensive dreams are soon forgotten during the waking hours.

You will also need a dream dictionary and I personally found the books written by Nerys Dee were more suited to my dreams.

Because dream books are written by different authors, they do not always reveal the same dream meanings, so it would be advisable to select a dream dictionary you feel comfortable with and use no other.

Once you have selected your own dictionary, you can then formulate a system for your own dream diary.

Nerys Dee's book entitled '**Understanding Dreams: What they are and how to interpret them'** (ISBN 9780007812073) is highly recommended.

Once you start keeping notes, you will eventually become more aware of the nature of your dreams and will be able to recognise the difference between ordinary dreams and spiritual ones.

A spiritual dream often left me with an elated feeling when I woke up.

Chapter Four

The Missing Studio

After leaving college in the early summer of 1972, I was employed as a commercial artist at a riveting firm for 15 months. This job, illustrating riveting guns and drafting out manuals did not have much scope and I soon felt the need to look for another occupation offering a more extensive and satisfying range of artistic creativity.

In the autumn of 1973, I saw an advert in the local paper for a typographic designer's job at a studio by the name of Gascoigne Lamb Ltd and I felt that this would be more suited to my talent.

A typographic designer's job was an essential occupation in the pre-computer era. If a client required a brochure, it would be my job to make a dummy mock up so that the client could see a visual image. Once this coloured draft had been agreed upon and accepted, the estimator would then be able to work out the cost of printing.

Upon seeing the advert for Gascoigne Lamb Ltd, I immediately wrote out an application and that same evening Dad suggested that we jump into the car and drive over to the studio and post the envelope by hand. Mum, Dad and I set off full of anticipation, but we could not find the place, we travelled backwards and forwards, up and down the road looking for this studio. Finally we had to give up and put the application into a Royal Mail post box. Two days later, I got a telephone call inviting me to call in for an interview as soon as it was convenient.

This worried Mum a lot because we had not been able to find the place, and she also felt that the request for an interview had come far too quickly and seriously she had visions of me being whipped off into some kind of white slave trade. But she need not have worried, the studio was set up inside a terrace house with a small plaque at the door, (no wonder we couldn't find it). The lounge downstairs was converted into a reception area and the boss along with his assistant worked on their drawing boards upstairs in what was supposed to be the main bedroom. After seeing my portfolio I was offered the job and a drawing board was set up for me in the spare bedroom. My boss was a gentleman who turned out to be very much like a father to me, more to the point, he was conscious of my verbal communication errors and would often help by correcting any misspoken words I should utter.

He was also concerned about my social life.

Should I mix more with the deaf people or the hearing people?

With both choices there was something of a dilemma.

I would encounter problems when I visited the local deaf club. Sign language was their main source of communication and because this type of interaction had been banned at Odsal House School, I couldn't participate as much as I would have liked to. At the same time, I found it very hard to follow group conversations with the hearing people and often found myself feeling left out.

My boss advised me to persevere with the hearing people so that they could help rectify any misspoken words I should inadvertently utter. It was necessary for me to improve my oral communication as I would be conversing with the studio clients.

I did keep in touch with some of my friends who were deaf, but soon found myself fading away from the deaf club as I socialised more with the hearing world. I would avoid large groups, finding it easier to mix with no more than four people, and having by now retired from running, I continued to enjoy other sporting activities such as table tennis, badminton, going to the gym and learning to swim.

I also took an interest in Yoga and I found this pastime very relaxing. To help enhance mindfulness, I would often sit in front of a candle flame. This specific training would have me gazing at the flame for two minutes before placing my hands over my eyes. Keeping my eyes open in the darkness created by the palms of my hands, a reflective image of the flame would then slowly appear and the purpose of this exercise was to fully concentrate on nothing but the image of the flame. If I controlled my thoughts, the image would intensify into a vibrant flame, but if my thoughts started to wander, the flame would disappear.

One evening when I was deep into this meditation experiment, I unknowingly scared the living daylights out of Mum.

Apparently, she had popped her head round my door and found my bedroom to be in total darkness apart from the glow of one candle flame illuminating yours truly sitting on the floor in a half lotus position with hands over my eyes (I could never do the full lotus). The shock of seeing me in this position caused her to go into panic mode and wondering what on earth I was doing, she ran back downstairs and into the lounge, shrieking to Dad and Christine, "I don't know what Katie is bringing into the house!"

We had a good laugh over this, after all was explained.

In 1974, Gascoigne Lamb Ltd moved out of the terrace house into a purpose built studio within the premises of an associated printing company and it was not long after that my boss decided to retire and live in Devon. I missed him a lot but we kept in touch by post until the correspondence dwindled down over the years to an annual letter in a Christmas card. I did visit him once in Devon and we occasionally telephoned each other.

The year 1976 saw the birth of my niece Claire just in time for Mum to hold her before she passed away. Sadly, Mum was a victim of cancer, but unbeknown to me at the time, what was about to happen was to be my spiritual awakening.

It was nine days after she died and the funeral had been and gone and things were beginning to settle down. Dad was worn out and Christine suggested that he go back home with her to Sidcup in Kent for a much needed rest and break. Although he and Christine were concerned about leaving me, I encouraged him to go, convincing him that I would be alright because I had to go to work anyway which also meant that I would not be spending all my time alone in the house. When I got home from work that same day, my family had already left and I walked into an empty house, but had a very strong feeling that Mum was around. What happened that evening was something I will never forget.

The Yoga meditation exercise was to prove useful.

I went to bed and set the alarm, noticing the time was 10.15 pm. I then slipped under the covers, turned off the light and closed my eyes. As I was drifting off to sleep, I lay there hoping Mum was alright, then two words came loud and clear inside my head, "Concentrate, Concentrate." It felt like I was receiving some kind of instruction to clear away all wandering thoughts. Then I physically felt a cold sharp blast of air at the back of my head and immediately after this, Mum's face appeared in full colour, clear and vivid in my third eye area, just above the nose. She was younger and wearing the blue spiked glasses she had worn about 20 years before. More to the point, she was smiling and happy. At seeing this, I instantly opened my eyes and felt total peace. It was then I knew she was all right. I looked at the alarm clock and it was only 10.30 p.m. The clear vision I had had was definitely no dream nor a figment of my imagination.

That cold, sharp blast at the back of my head was felt with such force and it was definitely no draught.

At that time I had very little knowledge of clairaudience or clairvoyance and the experience left me wondering what had actually happened.

In 1978, Dad married my stepmum Myra, and Big Grandma passed to spirit later that same year.

Facts, Theories and Anomalies relating to this Chapter

Subject – Spirit Communication, Meditation.

I would now like to fast forward to the year 2000 when I had the most extraordinary message during a clairaudient demonstration from a medium at a seminar. This message was referring to my former boss and below is my report which was written down very soon after the actual communication while the memory of it was still fresh in my mind.

"On Saturday 25th November 2000, I attended a clairaudient demonstration at a weekend seminar at Cober Hill, Cloughton near Scarborough. The medium asked me if the name 'Gascoigne' meant anything to me. I replied 'Yes' then she joked and said, 'I don't mean Paul Gascoigne[1]'. I laughed and said, 'No, but the name 'Gascoigne' does mean something to me.' The medium then said, 'Well, the gentleman here wants me to tell you that he is now over on the other side.' (meaning the Spirit World). I was shocked to hear this message thinking that this could not be right as my previous boss of Gascoigne Lamb Ltd was still alive on the earth plane.

As soon as I arrived home on Sunday 26th November, I telephoned him and was surprised to receive a recorded message saying, "The number you have dialled has not been recognised." Not knowing any other contact related to my former boss, I decided to send him an early Christmas card telling him that I tried to ring him and asking if everything was alright. I also wrote my home address on the card and on the envelope in the hope of receiving some kind of feedback.

The Christmas card was posted to Devon on 4th December. On the 18th December, I received a letter from his son in Yorkshire. He wrote: 'Dear Katie, I am sorry to tell you my father died on the 17th November.'

This message left me staggered. My boss had died only 8 days before I received that clairaudient communication on 25th November. As I did not know, obviously, telepathy was in no way involved Also he was the sort of man who would keep you informed of anything important.

This was another unexpected piece of brilliant evidential spirit communication.

------- 000 -------

---

1. Paul Gascoigne was a well-known footballer at the time.

How to Meditate

Many of my friends have told me that they are unable to meditate because there is far too much to think about. Life is too demanding and everyday affairs and background noises are a big distraction.

In today's busy world, there is a need to take time out and meditate, and by this, I don't mean sitting for hours on end in a lotus position with thumbs touching the middle finger whilst listening to the sound of your own 'Ohm'.

Yes – maybe that is what the master Yogis do, – a very high skill if you wish to go that far, but what is really needed in our everyday life is some form of focus. And 'Mindfulness' is often used as a practice today. It is a form of self-order to slow down all those cluttering thoughts and still the mind.

This is my way of meditating and I often feel a pleasant light tingling around the head afterwards.

The best way to start is to sit for about fifteen minutes which can be extended to a longer phase as you learn how to meditate comfortably according to your needs.

Find a comfortable chair and sit upright with your feet firmly on the ground and place your hands on your lap with your fingers entwined. Have the tip of your thumb touching the other thumb tip and relax. (I also like to have the tips of my little fingers touching as well.)

Close your eyes and think of every muscle in your body. If you feel any tension, let it go, let it drop and then take in a deep breath through the nose and hold it for a second or two and breathe out slowly through the mouth.

Breathe in peace, hold it and breathe out all the tension.

As your breathing becomes calm and slow, focus on your thumb and little finger tips. Concentrate on those and visualise energy flowing through them.

Visualise the air you breathe in as a pure white light entering into your being and flowing through your thumb and finger tips then around your body. Feel your body slowly filling up with white light at every deep breath starting from your feet to your knees, then up to your waist, up to your chest and up to your head. Concentrate on your crown chakra at the top of your head and feel the love of spirit reaching down to you.

Enjoy the spirit energy filling you up with goodness and love until you are ready to slowly return to earth and open your eyes.

Should you find it hard to visualise, then may I suggest another way of meditating by sitting comfortably in front of a flower and keeping your eyes open. This time, relax and concentrate on the flower; smell its aroma; observe its beauty; look deep into its petals; study the delicate veins and marvel at its incandescent colour. As you forget yourself by becoming really absorbed in the flower, you will become that flower, and be part of it and in return it will give you a moment of blissful peace and tranquillity.

Many people like to relax by listening to soft music or to a meditation CD, something like a gentle voice guiding them through a small gate and then into a beautiful garden.

Or, you could even try the candle flame experiment as mentioned earlier in this chapter.

There are many different ways of meditating to help you to drift into that deeper state of consciousness and in my case; this is when I would see the pictures as you will read about in the next chapter.

Chapter Five

The Book that Found Me

My career as a typographic designer was a busy one and I often found myself working long hours and at weekends to meet continuous deadlines.

Dad was now living with my stepmum Myra.

That left me as the only resident in the family home giving me the opportunity to relax, meditate and ponder over the mysteries of life. As I continued to wonder why we are here. I never ever forgot that fantastic experience of seeing Mum just nine days after she had passed to spirit.

That unforgettable spontaneous encounter accompanied by the distinctive and unusual sharp blast at the back of my head prompted me to ask more questions. A friend of mine told me that this was how mediums could see people through the third eye, but still oblivious to this suggestion, I carried on researching different religions by attending various denominations and to my disappointment, none provided any answers to my questions.

Although I started to wonder about Spiritualism, I hadn't the courage to investigate it. I was frightened of the unknown and had a fear of becoming possessed by some kind of unwanted entity.

That was until I had a very clear and simple dream.

I was looking at a window and all I could see through the glass was a stunning white light and the plain blue carpet below just left me in awe. It was the most beautiful blue I had ever seen. After I woke up, I looked into the meaning of all this in my dream book.

The dream symbolised protection; healing; Spiritual awareness and elevated consciousness to take place in the future.

I do remember waking up to a feeling of joy after that dream, but shrugged my shoulders and thought – now what?

Quite soon after, a colleague at work suggested I visit her sister Angela Clark.

Why?

Because at that time I wasn't feeling all that well and with Angela being a homeopathic consultant, my colleague thought she might be able to perk me up a bit?

So I decided to try her out and after a few successful sessions, a friendship grew and I soon found my feet under the table talking to her husband John who happened to be a Spiritual healer.

Well, this was interesting and at that point, I plucked up the courage to discuss Spiritualism and when John heard that my sister Christine lived in Guildford, he advised me to visit the nearby Harry Edwards Spiritual Healing Sanctuary.

On my next trip to Christine's for a holiday, I told her that I would like to visit this place in the hope of healing my deafness and my brother-in-law immediately objected to my going. He was very concerned about my safety, because to his way of thinking, such a sanctuary was a cult and Christine put his mind at rest by reassuring him that she would go with me.

When we arrived at this large house surrounded by idyllic gardens, we had nothing to fear as I was invited to sit down and take healing. I felt a strange tingling of energy as the two healers focused on me and I did, at the time, wonder what was happening.

It was a unique experience which left Christine and me with a great deal to discuss before we decided to drive over to a nearby village for cream teas. Sitting at the tea-place table, Christine said, "Well, can you hear me?" and my reply was, "Pardon?", and I can remember us both laughing about that, especially with me having had healing to help cure my deafness. At that point I did begin to wonder if it was my Karma that I should remain deaf and that there was a reason for it? The added question was, did I really want to be cured when the deficiency helped me to become what I am now?

However, I did make two more trips to the healing sanctuary and continued with absent healing for a while. There was no improvement in my hearing, but strangely enough, something unexpected was about to be cured and that was my fear of Spiritualism.

One day, when travelling back home from Christine's, the coach broke down on the motorway and whilst waiting for the relief transport, I started to read a Spiritualist magazine I had picked up from the sanctuary. After a short while, I heard a lady's voice saying,

"Are you into all that stuff?" She made me jump right out of my skin and when I looked up, I saw two ladies stood up leaning over the back of my seat glancing at the magazine. Not knowing what to say, I replied in a sheepish way, "Well, sort of." These two ladies then started to tell me about Spiritualist Churches confirming that there was nothing to be afraid of and they recommended a Spiritualist Church on Leeds Road in Huddersfield.

Well, I had visited various religious organisations looking for answers without success and a Spiritualist church was one I hadn't checked out.

I eventually plucked up the courage to go to the Huddersfield Spiritualist Church that they had recommended, and feeling quite apprehensive, I actually stopped outside the threshold wondering if I should really go in.

Following some hesitation, I slowly put my head through the open doorway to look around. Then a kindly gentleman who saw me came up and introduced himself as Harold, he gave me a lovely warm greeting and escorted me in.

The first thing that struck me was an almost full church and I was offered a seat even though some people were standing.

I sat there thinking, "Nothing spooky about this place." The organist was playing cheerful music, people were chatting away and the atmosphere was very relaxed indeed. Even the lady I was sat next to started talking to me and when I told her it was my very first visit, she immediately said, "Oh, you will like it here," explaining that they start off with prayers and songs, then there would be a session of philosophy, followed by communication with the spirit people.

What really fascinated me was that the philosophy came from the heart of the speaker and was not recited from a book. The spirit communication was interesting to listen to and although I didn't get a message, I was keen to visit the Church again.

I had been going to Yoga classes and now knowing how to meditate, I would often relax at home sitting comfortably listening to classical music. One day, whilst in this state of bliss with my eyes closed, a picture of a boy riding a bike flashed through. This spontaneous vision which was in colour and clear enough to register caused me to open my eyes, wondering what it was.

Why would I want to see a boy riding a bike?

I was simply listening to the music and I knew it wasn't my

imagination. Neither was it a dream and it certainly wasn't created by my own thought. These 'flash' pictures, some of them in colour and some of them like a negative image in black and white started to occur more often. They would not only happen when I meditated, but also when I was in bed drifting off to sleep. I would see spontaneous scenes like a white house among the fields; faces; a jogger in a 'T' shirt and shorts running towards me, etc.

I mentioned these strange experiences to my yoga teacher and he lent me a book entitled *'Fourteen Lessons in Yogi Philosophy and Oriental Occultism' by Yogi Ramacharaka'*. I took the book home and started to read it, but gave up after page 6 because I found it too hard to digest. When I returned the book politely explaining why I was bringing it back so soon, my yoga teacher told me not to worry because I was not ready for it just yet and that I would be able to understand its contents later on in life.

I also started to see spontaneous lights; they would vary in size from being as small as a pin prick to as large as 2cm diameter. I would be happily talking to someone and then suddenly I would see one or two of these lights. They were usually white or blue in colour and some would increase in size and then slowly disappear. The best one appeared as an orb of solid light approximately 2cms in diameter and it was electric-blue in colour. It did not move, but shone with such vibrancy, long enough for me to verify its presence. These lights never bothered me and I often wondered if they had anything to do with spirit?

After investigating a few other Spiritualist churches, I did find the communication with the spirit people variable according to the level of contact through the medium. Some were very good, but most provided messages that were far too vague and general for my liking. First names were often mentioned and I wasn't happy with just a single name unless there was further evidence to back it up. The name 'William' or 'Bill' kept cropping up claiming that he was helping me. This was all very nice, but I didn't know a William and I kept on wondering why Mum didn't come through. If she had the ability to show herself back in 1976, then why couldn't she relay a message through a medium?

My serious research continued to grow.

Building up more confidence, I took the opportunity to attended one or two open circles. These open circles which invited anyone to sit for the development of mediumship did not appeal to me because for some reason I felt very uncomfortable taking part in these gatherings. I didn't like the idea of sitting with people I did not know.

The Huddersfield Spiritualist Church held monthly discussion groups which I did enjoy. These were organised by an elderly couple named Robert and Georgina Brake – known to friends as Bob and Ena – and when we gathered together once a month, I would ask questions like there was no tomorrow. One particular question was, "What is the difference between Psychism and Spiritualism?" and that crucial question was the turning point which led to me being invited to Bob and Ena's home because Bob sensed I was very keen to know more.

Unbeknown to me then, we were to become great friends and I ended up visiting their home at least once a week borrowing books that could expand my knowledge. One day, a few years later, Ena picked up a book, looked at its cover and held it in the air saying to Bob, "I think Katie is ready for this one." It was entitled '*Fourteen Lessons in Yogi Philosophy and Oriental Occultism*' by Yogi Ramacharaka.

Facts, Theories and Anomalies relating to this Chapter

Subject – Healing, Yogi Philosophy, Possible Clairvoyance and Spirit Lights.

It would appear that I was destined to read that book and by then, I could digest its contents and it certainly helped me to understand the difference between Psychism and Spiritualism – or should I say Psychism and Spiritualist mediumship.

Ena did not encourage participating in open circles mainly because when sitting with strangers you do not know what kind of energies you are mixing with. So as it happened, my intuition regarding the open circle was right. In my opinion, it is always safer to sit with people you know and if you do choose to sit in an open circle, do make sure it is in the presence of an experienced medium.

As I have got older, the flash images and the spirit lights do not occur as often. Perhaps it is because I have less energy or it could be that I am now more preoccupied with material matters such as writing books. I do not meditate as much as I use to, so that could be another reason for the decline in such experiences.

The so-called spirit lights were not the streaks of flashing/floating ones that one sees when experiencing a migraine. Definitely they were solid orbs of vibrancy that stayed in one place in mid air and often swelled out to become larger before disappearing when I tried to focus on them.

I was to later realise that we do periodically go astray on our path of life, but once back on the right track, a pattern in the form of a plan somehow seems to make itself known.

For example, after I had the dream about the window, how was I to know that I would be visiting a Homeopathic consultant which led to me meeting John who advised me to go to the Healing Sanctuary?

If I had not picked up the Spiritualist magazine at the sanctuary, the two ladies, (complete strangers on a coach) would not have spoken to me about the Huddersfield Spiritualist Church, a place where I was to meet Bob and Ena and attend the discussion groups. Eventually they were to become my mentors in my research which would enhance my interest in physical phenomena and lead me to the Stewart Alexander Home Circle where I was to become an honorary member.

If you can convince me that this destiny wasn't planned in the Spirit World – then I will eat my hat.

Referring to the difference between Psychism and Spiritualist mediumship, my conclusion, as I understand it is:

– a psychic person who can read minds and auras is not necessarily a medium and will have no connection with the Spirit World.

– a genuine medium – Spiritualist or not – is able to connect and communicate with the spirit people, even when the recipient on Earth is miles or kilometres away.

Recommended books relating to this chapter

For readers wishing to go deep into the entire field of the Yogic Philosophy with its teachings of Mental and Spiritual Principals; the Human Aura; Thought Dynamics; Telepathy; Clairvoyance; Psychic Influence; The Astral World; Spiritual Evolution and much more, I recommend...

'Fourteen Lessons in Yogi Philosophy' by Yogi Ramacharaka (ISBN 9780997414837)

For those who prefer a much lighter read, *'The Boy Who Saw True'* (ISBN 9781844131501), is unique.

This classic book is the diary of a young Victorian boy born with clairvoyance with the ability to see auras. Enjoy reading about his experiences and his writing about such things like his worried mother taking him to have his eyes tested because he saw dead people and the amusing banters with his older sister will make you smile. (The book even includes his spelling mistakes which may make you chuckle even more).

Chapter Six

Expecting Mum?

My confidence in Spiritualism had certainly grown, and by now, I had a better understanding of what happened when I saw Mum after she had died back in 1976. Even so, I still failed to understand why Mum did not communicate through platform mediums.

I needed to investigate further and decided to do more research, this time with private sittings.

My first took place on 14th March 1990.

This reading turned out to be very successful and my records show that during the forty-minute session, there were twenty-five definite connections, four possible connections and four no connections. Sadly there was no mention of Mum.

I have to admit that I was impressed with this particular sitting and on top of that, my sister Christine also decided to have a reading with the same medium.

She too was amazed and below is her account. (Christine was very close to Little Grandma, my mother's mother).

"The medium said 'I have a lady here – oh! She is so tiny – she is like a little bird. She says she is your Granny – oh oops, I have gone and put my foot in it, she is quite cross with me. She says she is your GRANDMA!! She is with Jack.'

That is when I realised that this was true – Grandma had always insisted we call her Grandma and not Granny, Nanny, Nan etc., – she really hated those other names and when she hated something there was no trying to get her to change her mind and also Granddad's name was John (known as Jack).

The reason I remember the above so very clearly is that the significance of it was absolutely printed on my mind. Also, he can't have been reading my mind as some people claim mediums do, as I was not thinking of Grandma at all, in fact I was very much hoping that Mum would come."

Christine had also been hoping that Mum would come through but there was no mention of her in that reading.

The one thing I liked about my private sitting was that I had a recording of it all on cassette tape and this enabled me to categorise in writing the definite connections, possible connections and no connections.

Much later on, some of the 'no connections' that did not mean anything to me at the time would make sense, and more to the point, this type of confirmation certainly ruled out telepathy.

Facts, Theories and Anomalies relating to this Chapter

Subject – Spirit Communication

Even after starting my intensive research, I was still expecting Mum to communicate through various mediums but for some reason she never did.

This would bring me to the point of further questioning.

I knew of people who had experienced similar disappointing situations, especially when their so-called deceased loved ones had promised to make contact after death but failed to do so.

Then, why (in many cases) didn't they communicate?

Chapter 2 tells of a successful communication via the psychic drawings of three spirit people but not Mum or Grandma.

Chapter 4 tells of a highly evidential clairaudient message from a deceased colleague but not Mum.

Thinking about it, if the mediums had brought Mum through, then I would have dismissed the message as telepathy, so it now comes to light that there is more to consider than meets the eye.

It is worth noting that evidence of spirit people not in your thoughts at the time of the communication can prove to be rather staggering, just as much as Christine's reading was to her.

I was to learn something here – never expect to hear what you are hoping to hear because invariably you will only end up being disappointed. It is my belief that intense thoughts on hoping to communicate with a particular (deceased) person can create a blockage, so much so, it can obstruct the true elements of the reading itself.

There are various reasons why our close (so called deceased) loved ones do not communicate and possible suggestions are mentioned in my book, *'Touching the Next Horizon'* but for now, let's stay with the subject of understanding why it is so important to keep an open mind.

------- 000 -------

Keeping a Record of your Readings

There are several things you need to be aware of when attending a reading.

1. Do not give away any personal information to the medium.
2. Always keep an open mind.

3. Do not turn the reading into something you want to hear.
4. Guard your facial expressions.

Different mediums have their own ways of working; for example some could ask too many questions and if this is the case, then your best policy would be is to say nothing but yes or no. More to the point – be careful not to feed the medium by disclosing any hints of personal information.

The best evidential messages are the ones that don't mean anything to you at the time, but when the significance comes to light at a later date. This will certainly rule out telepathy and the only way to realise this is by keeping a record in writing.

My written records were very intense, to such a degree that I would number each line of the reading and scrutinise every detail, but you don't have to do this.

Just noting down the interesting bits of your reading might be sufficient, (even when something doesn't mean anything to you at the time), and then itemise the details into 3 categories.

1. Definite connections
2. Possible connections
3. No connections

Keep a file of these categories and in days, months or even in the future you may come across astounding links to the 'No Connections' category. This happened to me as you will read about in the next chapter.

Keeping a record on paper is good for researching and I find it so much easier to track something in writing rather than having to spend hours re-listening to a long recording.

But please be aware of becoming addicted to too many readings, particularly when you are desperately eager for a message you want to hear. This is not a healthy practice. Researching into the mysteries of the consciousness is one thing; not being able to move on in life is another.

During my research, I did experience a lot of cold readings, and by this I mean a fraudulent clairaudient medium can bluff such messages by closely observing and reading the faces of the audience. Such a medium has only got to mention a name and then will look out for a gasp or shocked expression from any member of the audience. This will enable the medium to home in on that particular person and start asking discreet questions leading on to personal clues. Do be careful not to become a gullible recipient especially when you are grieving.

------- OOO -------

Recommended books relating to this chapter

You can read more about my research and the possible reasons as to why it is difficult for some spirit people to communicate in:

'Touching the Next Horizon' by Katie Halliwell (ISBN 9781908421470)

'Love Dad: How My Father Died... Then Told Me He Didn't.' by Mike Anthony (ISBN 9781951805661) is an excellent book detailing how Mike's own research turned his sceptical mind into accepting life after death.

Chapter Seven

The Unknown Connection

I mentioned in Chapter Five that various platform mediums brought up a 'William or Bill', and because this name did not mean anything to me I decided to check out my family tree. There were a few 'Williams' and the nearest to me was Grandma Halliwell's father (my Great Granddad), but even then, I felt it was far too distant and too vague to be accepted as a clear-cut spirit contact.

That was until a particular private sitting on 22 April 1990 which also brought up the name 'William'.

I knew very little about my Grandma's people until Auntie Bessie (Grandma's niece), filled me in with further information about her side of the family.

Looking into the details of this particular reading, I was to discover that both the medium and I made mistakes, which I think is something every researcher should be aware off.

Below is a section of a transcript from the recording. The medium's words are printed in italic and mine are printed in capital letters: -

As I start to get a contact with spirit, I am watching a lady come to me, as the lady comes – tell me have you a brother?

NO

I am conscious as I make a link with this lady, she is talking to me, and she is talking about her son as she comes, and I know this as I am getting into contact with her, did you know your father's mother?

YES

Was there at anytime to do with your father's people, anybody that lived either where it was rural, or where there's been a small holding?

I'M SORRY? WHERE THERE'S BEEN A...?

A small holding, like a small farm, because this lady takes me back and she takes me to where ... countryside. It seems to be open where I am looking, and I know that she is speaking, so I am conscious that this is a grandmother to you and will you know William?

WOULD I KNOW...?

William. Who's Bill?

(Hesitating) - I DON'T KNOW HIM PERSONALLY.

There's somebody she speaks of named Bill and she is talking with Tom and I am very aware of where someone passed with cancer. Who had cancer? Who passed with cancer?

ARE YOU TALKING ABOUT MY GRANDMOTHER'S SIDE? (CHECKING THIS OUT BECAUSE I WAS THINKING MUM HAD CANCER).

It is something to do with a man; it's something to do with a man.

(MY THOUGHTS THEN SWITCHED OVER TO UNCLE ARNOLD MENTIONED IN CHAPTER 2).

I will stop there now because I would like to discuss this part of the reading.

When the medium asked if I had a brother, I lost confidence in him straight away and I also thought he was asking far too many questions, so I was on my guard and did my utmost not to feed him with any information.

As a result of this fifteen minute reading, there were twenty-four definite connections, eight possible connections and four no connections.

During a private sitting like this one where names are mentioned, I would try to think of somebody I personally know and in this case, it apparently caused some confusion because the medium kept referring back to my Grandma's side of the family.

Further into the reading, more names relating to Grandma were also mentioned and Harold was one of them. He was Grandma's brother, (the same gentleman shown in photograph 1 on page 24).

So, referring to the medium's first question, was this 'the brother' he was talking about – not my brother, but Grandma's?

And what about William?

Was this particular William my Great Grandfather?

I still wasn't sure.

As usual, my thoughts during the sitting were focused on Mum and it wasn't until much later on that I realised that Grandma was talking about her life on earth and not mine. She was talking about her people – not the people I know.

How self -centred my thoughts had been!

Facts, Theories and Anomalies relating to this Chapter

Subject – Spirit Communication

This is a prime example of not being on the same thought wave length with the spirit people. I was SO set in my mind hoping Mum would come through, and had I been less focussed on her it is possible that the reading could have been more fluent.

With this in mind, I decided to investigate deeper into Grandma Halliwell's family history. I knew she had a brother and that they were both born in Doncaster with most of the family employed as railway people. What I did not know, was that Grandma's side of the family originated in Lincolnshire.

My Great Grandfather William's family were agricultural labourers and William's father was also a farm worker before he moved to Doncaster, hence explaining this part of the reading:

"Was there at anytime to do with your father's people, anybody that lived either, where it was rural, or where there's been a small holding?"

The reason why I knew so little of William was that Big Grandma kept largely tight-lipped regarding her parents. It was a family secret, something not to be talked about in her day. It turns out that both her parents were born out of wedlock and although Grandma did talk about her mother, she said very little about her father, William. I was to discover that he had left his wife for another woman and this did not work out for him, but in time, his forgiving family accepted him back into the fold.

And there is further evidence regarding Grandma's people.

Allow me to repeat this part of the reading:

"...somebody she speaks of named Bill and she is talking with Tom..."

I was to find out more about the family.

Grandma's brother; (my Great Uncle Harold) had a son also called Harold, but the family always referred to him as Tom, (a pet name, that I would not find in the family tree). Unbeknown to me at the time of the reading, which was 22nd April 1990, Tom had passed over in January that very same year.

The medium then asked who had cancer and my thoughts wrongly focused on Mum and Uncle Arnold – this obviously broke the connection with Grandma's people. I just wasn't tuned in and I was to later find out that Tom's younger brother died before him – of cancer.

This extra evidence of Tom and his younger brother (both Grandma's nephews) and Harold being Grandma's brother (all within her family) did make me wonder if the said William might have been my Great Grandfather.

Who knows?

Changing the subject and referring back to the 'brother' scenario. When the medium asked if I had a brother, it could have been Grandma telling him that she had a brother. This brings about the fact that some messages are not always interpreted correctly by the medium.

A very similar thing happened in the year 2006 when I received a spirit communication from another excellent medium. He had a message for me from Grandma and told me that he clearly heard the word 'big'. He then went on to say, "So she must have been a large lady?"

I knew straight away that this was a misinterpretation on his part because he heard the word 'big' and assumed that she was large. It is important that mediums should only relay what they hear, as I always called her Big Grandma – not that she was a large person, but that she was tall and slim.

So many mediums do forget to simply give what they get and they should not interpret, as the unique message can be very relevant to the recipient.

Clairaudient/clairvoyant mediums can and do make these mistakes and it would be advisable to be aware of such misconceptions.

That same medium then continued with Grandma's message – she wanted me to write about my life story.

Was this book that you are now reading, destined to be written?

Who knows?

Incidentally, since I began to acknowledge William as my Great Grandfather and sending him my loving thoughts, the name William or Bill has never ever come up again and I like to think that he has now moved on.

Also, I began to realise that it was high time I stopped those blinkered thoughts of expecting Mum to communicate and focus on understanding the Spirit World with the intention of helping others.

Since then, with the right kind of thought conditions, Mum has often communicated.

Here is one example:

I am fast forwarding to 4th May 2000 when Christine and I sat in a séance with the Stewart Alexander Circle. Walter (one of Stewart's main spirit guides) is a Canadian who died in 1911 and he is speaking on behalf of Mum through Stewart in trance.

At that time, Christine lived on a narrowboat and unbeknown to me, she would often wonder what Mum would think of her small makeshift ironing board fitted into the boat (because Mum use to be extremely meticulous with her own ironing). Here is the transcript of the recording from my book 'Touching the Next Horizon'.

Walter. Ok. Ok. Ok. Your mother brings her love to you both.

Christine. Oh, thank you, Mum, love.

W. Ok. Ok. Tell me something – Did she... What is this regarding ironing? Hmmm?

Katie. Ironing?

W.– Yes, was she particularly...

Chr. Yes

W. – careful?

Chr. Yes, yes.

W. You know what I'm saying here?

Chr. Yes she was, yes.

W. She says she's trying to bring some evidence to you of her presence here this evening. She's saying that I must mention this to you both. Hmmm?

Chr. I've been thinking of her while I've been ironing. Yes.

W. I hope therefore that this proves to you, Chris, how close your loved ones who are now in my world are - how close they are to you all.

Chr. Oh bless them, I know.

W. You send out a thought and they receive, hmmm?

Chr. Thank you. Mum.

K. Thank you.

W. Ok, Ok, Ok. She's saying if only once again she could hold you both.

K. That'd be nice.

Chr. That would be lovely.

W. But you know... but you know that she still loves you in the way that she always did.

Chr. Bless her.

K. She's always in our thoughts.

W. And you in hers, ma'am. This is a time to rejoice!

Everyone. Yes. Yes.

You can listen to the recording of above transcript on-line (available at the time of printing) and hear Walter's Canadian accent, which is totally different to Stewart's own voice, by visiting:

www.alexanderproject.bandcamp.com

To hear the above, make sure you are on the <u>audio</u> tab and select Track 13.

Chapter Eight

The Hospice

By the end of 1990 Dad had been diagnosed with cancer and my stepmum Myra being 79 years of age was struggling to provide the specialist care he needed. Eventually he was admitted to a hospice and on arrival found a loving and caring atmosphere offering every possible aspect of dignity. It was an eye opener for me and little did I know then that I was to play a big part in connection with this wonderful place of love, peace and harmony.

As the hospice was not easily accessible from Myra's home, I found myself transporting her over to visit Dad most evenings and because I had to drive straight from work with no time for a meal, Myra would prepare a sandwich for me to eat in the hospice dining room. This worked well, because it gave her the chance be alone with Dad in his room and at the same time, it gave me the opportunity to meet and chat with the other residential patients.

Finding the hospice an absolute haven for those in need and being in awe of the care and support it had to offer, I decided to do some voluntary work as a trolley lady serving tea, coffee and biscuits to the patients and their visitors.

The trolley rota meant that there would be certain times when I would be in the hospice without Dad knowing. One day I found him sitting alone in the small chapel, which was unusual because he was not a religious person and most certainly not a church goer. Obviously he had had a change of heart and I decided not to disturb him, but at the same time I wondered what prompted him to make such a move.

Was it perhaps fear of the unknown?

I can only guess.

During his earthly life, Dad thought my quest for knowledge about the Spirit World was absolute nonsense. However, when his health was finally failing, I managed to discreetly mention that if he did happen to see any deceased loved ones, such as Mum, Granddad or Grandma then he should not hesitate to go with them. He told me that he did not want to leave Myra and I promised him that I would take care of her in Jill's absence, for at that time Myra's daughter Jill, was living in Saudi Arabia. This gave Dad some comfort despite the fact that he was completely oblivious to the unknown adventure ahead of him – his inevitable destination.

After Dad had passed away peacefully on April 20th 1991, I continued with my hospice charitable work, this time, not only being on trolley duty, but helping with the day care patient gatherings and also participating in the bereavement support group meetings. My typographic talents were put to good use as I voluntarily designed brochures, leaflets and any promotional literature for this much needed place.

I also continued to visit the hospice patients as often as possible and would spend many an hour chatting to a lady residing there (to protect her identity, I shall refer to her as Jean). She would sit by the window and greet people with a lovely smile and chat to them, directing any new visitors towards the whereabouts of their residential friends or relatives. She was also brilliant at putting new patients at ease. One day I came in for trolley duty and saw Jean looking ever so cross and I asked her what the matter was. "It's that Catholic priest!" she grumbled. "He walks in and never says hello to anyone. He just storms straight through and never acknowledges anyone except those of his own flock. It is very bad manners!"

As she sat there looking so grumpy, my response was, "Well Jean, not everyone is as nice as you." She looked at me and muttered the word, "Catholicism!" with a strong feeling of disgust, then pointed her finger at me with a stern warning, "And there is something much worse than Catholicism," she remarked very seriously. I curiously asked her what this would be, and her reply was "Spiritualism."

Surprised at hearing this, my reply was simply "Oh."

I certainly knew not to let Jean find out about my research on life after death, but some of the nurses who did know about my quest were intrigued. They obviously couldn't talk about it because of patient confidentiality, but we did have discussions on what dying patients see and experience before leaving the physical body.

The voluntary work I was doing at the hospice made me aware of a unique state of consciousness. Entering the hospice was like walking into a totally different world where the madness of material activity outside had no chance of existing in this place of love and care. Almost every working day, I would be rushed off my feet desperately trying to meet printing deadlines and whenever I drove into the hospice car park, I would have to sit in the car for a good few minutes to slow myself down before merging into this peaceful and tranquil atmosphere.

It was so important to be on the same wavelength with the patients.

By now a lot of my spare time was concentrated on Myra and my voluntary work. This of course brought my regular visits to the Spiritualist church to an end, but I still continued to visit Bob and Ena.

While all this was happening, a disturbing change was hovering in the air. The printing company I worked for was to become a victim of modern technology. Most of our customers were now able to print their own promotional material and redundancy was inevitable. Some of our workforce had already been laid off and my turn unfortunately came in January 1992.

Ending up with no job gave me more time for voluntary work in the midst of seeking for new employment and some of the patients who knew of my fate did show concern. For example, a lady I shall call 'Eileen' had been for chemotherapy treatment and one day when I was on trolley duty, I literally failed to recognise this lady and walked straight past her. Her face looked completely different and she had lost so much hair. Later on, I sat beside her and held her hand and was utterly lost for words as she told me how she so wished she had never had the chemo done. Then out of the blue, she suddenly grasped my arm with her other hand and looked at me with such hope asking if I had found a job yet. Oh! I could have wept on the spot. Here was a lady dying of cancer and yet she thought of others rather than herself and was most concerned about me.

As for Jean, bless her, she kept telling me –"You will get through, you may not think so just now, but you will get through."

It was not long before I was offered a part-time paid job at the hospice overseeing the donated cash and monies coming in which included many trips to the bank. I felt very honoured and privileged to be trusted with such a responsibility and the patients who knew me showed their delight when they found out that I would be spending more time with them.

Once a year, the hospice would hold a garden party, and it was the usual custom to take the patients – those who were well enough–

around the stalls before the gates were opened. This gave them the opportunity to have first choice at purchasing anything that took their eye. Following one such event I arrived to count up the takings and on that occasion I was only just recovering from a bad head cold. Being careful not to pass it on to anyone inside the hospice, I looked through the window and told Jean that I was not coming in because I didn't want to spread any germs. However, Jean was very insistent, motioning for me to come inside and I had no choice but to approach her trying my best not to get too close. I then watched her delicate shaking hand go into her large bag to pull out a cake, and she handed it to me saying "I've bought this for you," and then with an authoritative voice made a firm statement, "Now! You go and see a doctor, that's what they are there for!"

I went back outside and marvelled at her strength of mind thinking to myself that although the patients may have failing material bodies, the love and care they could impress upon others was extremely remarkable. They knew how to share life and they certainly gave me the extra support I needed during my period of redundancy.

Facts, Theories and Anomalies relating to this Chapter.

Subject – Atmospheres, Dying and Bereavement.

Have you ever walked into a house and felt an atmosphere you either liked or disliked?

Have you ever noticed a dog suddenly backing away from entering a doorway or cowering in a corner for some unknown reason?

We all have this type of sense which often lies dormant and yet it is notably strong in animals. For example, they know to head off to higher ground long before humans realise that a tsunami is about to take place.

Walking into somewhere strange can trigger off this sense of feeling the atmosphere, and entering a hospice for the first time is bound to have a similar effect on many visitors. Feeling a totally different atmosphere from our busy material world can be quite unnerving. Thankfully, in such places there are some very special people. Nurses and volunteers, – beautiful souls – who create an aura of peace and harmony, and know how to help the patients' relatives and friends come to terms with what is happening to their lives. To me, they are angels in disguise offering such essential and much needed support.

Despite what is happening around you in a hospice, along with experiencing inevitable major changes in your life, it is a wonderful comfort to know that there is evidence of life after so called death. You may not feel it at the time of bereavement, but your so-called deceased loved one being only a thought away, will be much closer to you now than ever before.

Dad did come back to communicate occasionally, and on 15th March 2015 he told me (via a clairaudient medium) that he was surprised to see Mum when he passed over. This must have been quite bewildering for him as he did not want to leave Myra.

Myra thought a lot of Dad and after his death she asked me a question. "When I go to the Spirit World, I would like to be with your Dad, but how can I be with him when your Mum will be there?"

Myra passed to spirit in January 2007.

It might be of interest to know that I was also told by the above medium in the same sitting that Dad was being supported by both Mum and Myra who were working closely together to help him make contact through any mediumistic communication.

So, it is nice to know that even if you do get married more than once on Earth, it is love that blends us all together as one united whole in the Spirit World.

Incidentally, Jean never found out that I was a Spiritualist.

------- 000 -------

Recommended books relating to this chapter

'*Soul Messengers*' by Dr Annette Childs (ISBN 9781073099627) is a remarkable book, an excellent read about a true story detailing how a deceased wife manages to make spirit communication breakthroughs to her sceptic businessman husband and also stays in contact with the author.

'*Life in the World Unseen*' by Anthony Borgia (ISBN 9781544858302) is one of my favourite books explaining what life is like in the Spirit World. A book I would recommend to anyone.

Chapter Nine

The Little Square

It was quite a blow to be made redundant in January 1992 after eighteen years of employment at the printing company, and I did not have any success in finding a similar occupation. Sadly, computers had brought an end to the art and craft of designing printed promotional literature by hand.

The job at the hospice did help to keep my head above water, but a part time salary was not enough to live on, therefore, my search for full time employment continued.

I can remember having a private reading around mid 1992 and was told that I would be offered a job via a hand written letter. This, I thought was very strange because surely any correspondence offering employment would be typed on an official letterhead.

Myra, bless her heart, was constantly on the lookout hoping to find me a job and one day she spotted an advert in her local newspaper. It was for an administrative assistant at the Benefits Agency. My first reaction was to ignore it because it had nothing to do with typographic design or graphic art and the salary was less than a third of what I had previously been earning. However, since it was a full time job, it did offer more than I was earning at the hospice. Myra fully understood that it wasn't exactly what I was looking for and made a valid suggestion; "At least you could use it as a stepping stone until you find something more suitable."

I decided to give it a go by sending off an application and the outcome was an invitation to an administrative assistant test. The result turned out to be successful and I was placed on the reserve list. A little later, they offered me a temporary job for a few months, which I rejected because I had too much to lose with the permanent part time job I already held at the hospice.

Then a few weeks later, I received an unexpected request from the Benefits Agency's personnel department. A letter came through the post and when I opened it, I was astonished to find nothing but a lengthy hand written message on an official printed letterhead asking if I would be interested in a full time permanent job starting on January 3rd 1993. I was amazed at the offer, and that private reading, a few months earlier, telling me about a hand-written letter had turned out to be absolutely correct.

I accepted the job with the full intention of taking Myra's advice to treat it as a stepping stone and unbeknown to me at that time, that stepping stone was to be eighteen years long. I was destined to be employed by the Benefits Agency (now the Department of Work and Pensions) until the day I retired.

The Benefits Agency was certainly an eye opener. My customers were not the company executives I was accustomed to, but people who were struggling to make ends meet. It was such a contrast and I did sympathise with those individuals who were on the dole because I knew only too well what it was like to be without a job.

At the new office there was a fair amount of training involved and courses to attend, and much of my spare time was used up by revising and studying to expand my capabilities for different assignments. In addition to this, I found myself visiting Myra more often now that she was on her own and I really did enjoy her company. We got on extremely well together and enjoyed tripping off on various holiday ventures. Being quite occupied with the above commitments, I sadly had to give up my voluntary work at the hospice but I still managed to visit Bob and Ena.

My new job was definitely administrative, a far cry from the creative art work I had previously long enjoyed. But on the plus side, the Benefits Agency offered flexi time and the working hours were not as long. The training courses often saw me standing up and speaking in front of a group of colleagues and this was something I had never done before. I was also involved in writing reports.

I wonder now if this could have been planned, because it was excellent training for what was to come. At that time I had absolutely no idea that in about ten years' time I would be writing reports and books on Stewart Alexander's physical mediumship along with giving talks to audiences of up to ninety-plus people.

Facts, Theories and Anomalies relating to this Chapter.

Subject – Spirit Communication.

Returning to 1990, in my first private sitting (mentioned in Chapter 6) which took place on 14th March, I was told, *"no disrespect, your life is a little closed; it is like a little square that you move around in now."*

The spirit people, in a nice way, were trying to indicate that I was to move on, and at that time I did not suspect that redundancy would shortly be forced upon me.

I thought my career at the printing company was quite secure and I was happy in my own little studio coming up with ideas for promotional printed literature and I was oblivious to the threat of advancing computer technology. However, this inevitable shift was to help me progress in life.

As was politely pointed out, I was in actual fact, living in my own little square.

The same reading also carried hints of what was to happen.

"What you are doing, you are moving forward. Watch where there are outside forces or there are agencies of some kind that come in to help you and you must accept that help – don't push it to one side."

Although I did not understand it at the time – looking back, it seems to be relevant to what you have just read in this chapter, i.e. I wanted to ignore the advert for the Benefits Agency because it wasn't my profession and Myra was to suggest I use that job as a stepping stone.

There is so much more I would like to tell about this highly successful private reading I had on the 14th March 1990, but for now I would like to bring your attention to a particular part of the recording:

"All I find is the area of Hartshead all around me, so I want you to watch for links you will have with that area. They are good links, whatever they are, they are good, because as I stand at that point, I look around me and I can see houses in the distance, and I can also see green fields with open spaces. This green, that is attached to a link with Hartshead, indicates an enjoyment of some kind."

So – what was all this to do with Hartshead?

Chapter Ten

The Mystery Link

Christine and I found the name of Hartshead quite puzzling.

Why should this particular locale come up in the reading?

The enigma of it all prompted us to take a run out in the car and have a look at this place. When we arrived, we sat in our parked vehicle scanning the view only to find nothing of interest.

"Well? Have you got any vibes?" Christine asked.

"No," was my reply - "Do you feel anything?"

"No," said Christine.

We sat there viewing the surroundings and looking at each other until finally coming to the conclusion that nothing out of the ordinary was going to happen. Feeling disappointed at the outcome, we decided it was high time to go back home, but at least we enjoyed the run out.

What were we expecting?

I have no idea!

After the initial run out, I decided to study that bit of the reading again:

"All I find is the area of Hartshead all around me, so I want you to watch for links you will have with that area. They are good links, whatever they are, they are good, because as I stand at that point, I look around me and I can see houses in the distance, and I can also see green fields with open spaces. This green, that is attached to a link with Hartshead, indicates an enjoyment of some kind."

Hartshead borders the less prominent suburban area of Bradley and this is where Bob and Ena lived.

Although I am unable to exactly recall when I first met Bob and Ena, I do remember drinking tea with Ena and her friends in the refectory at Huddersfield Spiritualist Church before she introduced me to her husband Bob. This would be around October or November of 1989. The back end of that year would be about the time I started to attend their monthly discussion group meetings at the church.

The private sitting took place on 14th March 1990, a month or two before I was invited to their home. At the time of the reading, I did not know where they lived.

Bob and Ena celebrating their Golden Wedding on
2nd June 1991.

I now think the medium was directed to this certain area and he interpreted Hartshead simply because he knew of the place.

My understanding of Spirit contact through 'thought' is an instinctive motive with a tendency to communicate metaphorically. This is probably why green fields indicating an enjoyment of some kind was symbolically more favoured rather than using the spoken word – i.e. actual names and places. (Unbeknown to me then, I was to spend many a happy time with Bob and Ena).

Of course, it would have been more evidential to simply say that I would have links with Bob and Ena, but then, knowing me, I would have dismissed this as mind-reading or telepathy.

I was so glad I kept a detailed record of this private sitting because what didn't make sense at the time of the reading, did make sense later on.

Spirit messages can sometimes be quite puzzling and often in a very sensitive and private way because our paths and level of knowledge are unique to each and every one of us.

My path was to learn and understand more about spirit communication.

Bob and Ena had walked their own very interesting path and it came as no surprise why they were eager to pass on their first hand experiences. They had amassed an array of knowledge, and this is what, in my opinion, made them so special.

They were free spirits on this Earth plane and although they had been members of certain religions and organisations for a time, they were never tied down to any man-made beliefs, rules and regulations. Their freedom of thought was an eye opener for me, and I was to learn of many different aspects of various realities. Keeping an open mind was indeed important for my research.

The Silver Birch books of philosophy were favourite readings at the time and books on the White Eagle teachings were Bob's particular choice.

Bob and Ena's library was like an Aladdin's cave of knowledge, but there was one book I really enjoyed reading and that was 'On the Edge of the Etheric' by Arthur Findlay which enhanced a deeper interest in physical mediumship.

Bob and Ena often talked about their past lives, a subject not all Spiritualists accept and some of the church members who were limited to Spiritual Healing, Clairvoyance and Clairaudience apparently had little concept of physical phenomena.

I have to admit, that when Ena talked about her experience of physical mediumship, such as hearing the disembodied voice of her deceased mother speaking from the middle of the ceiling in a well-lit room, along with her detailed descriptions about spirit people materialising and actually walking out of a cabinet to touch the sitters, was to me at that time, hard to believe. Although I trusted Ena, I could not help thinking that it must have been her vivid imagination, but she would tell her accounts in such detail as if they happened only yesterday and Bob always confirmed that what she was telling me was true.

It was apparent that this type of mediumship was – and still is – rarely experienced. I also asked why such phenomena so often happened in the past rather than now.

Ena's answer to my question was that people do not have the time to sit in home circles[1] like they used to in her day. She would point to the television and simply say, "That is what has taken over, killing off the art of conversation and socialising, thus preventing friends from gathering together and building up an atmosphere with the possibility of forming a physical phenomena circle."

Bob and Ena also expressed caution about the danger in producing ectoplasm. If it was accidentally exposed to any form of unexpected light then the ectoplasm would shoot straight back into the medium and could cause a haemorrhage, or even death.

This was another reason why very few physical phenomena circles demonstrated in public.

Unless you have actually seen physical mediumship in action, it is very hard to accept that such phenomena does exist and I would sit in Bob and Ena's lounge repeatedly asking "Is all this really true?" to which they both confirmed with a definite yes.

What helped me come to terms with it all was a video they had of Minnie Harrison's physical mediumship. Minnie's son, Tom had prepared an hour-long film explaining what he personally witnessed at his mother's circle. Complete with good evidence and photographs of materialised spirit people, the video (now in DVD) entitled 'Visitors from the Other Side' is well worth watching.

Having seen this video, I was motivated to fire off another question:-

"Do you know if there are any physical mediums around these days?"

Bob and Ena showed me some literature confirming that there were a number of home circles in operation and this came in the form of the Noah's Ark Society Newsletters. This society (now defunct), supported physical mediumship and published reports on home circles around the country in the 1990s.[2]

One particular physical medium who was often mentioned in these newsletters was Stewart Alexander.

---

1. A home circle is a group of friends sitting for the development of either mental mediumship or physical phenomena.
2. These Newsletters, later known as *The Ark Review* are now available on the internet at - https://noahsarksocietyarchive.org

Facts, Theories and Anomalies relating to this Chapter.

Subject – Spirit Communication, Physical Mediumship.

Referring to the 'green fields' in the Hartshead reading, (indicating enjoyment of some kind), I really did value Bob and Ena's company and we spent many a happy time together throughout the 1990s setting off on trips to different spiritual gatherings. We would come home and discuss the outcome of our visit in comparison with Bob and Ena's vast knowledge of physical phenomena and spiritual philosophy.

This brings us to the subject of 'thought'. It is easier for the Spirit people to communicate in symbolic form because 'thought' has no verbal language. Below is an excerpt from my book, *'Touching the Next Horizon'*.

"The Spirit World is one of thought, where the etheric (spirit) body is free from the heavy and slow vibrations of our Earth plane. Freda (one of Stewart's main Spirit communicator's) once explained how she can travel from A to B in the blink of an eye; apparently she has only to think of a place, or a person, and she is there, or she is with them. Time and distance as we understand it, does not exist in the Spirit World. Freda knows about any event taking place simply through the attraction of thought.

"Author's note
Have you ever wondered about 'thought'?
What is it?
And where does it come from?
If you sit back and really think about this, it might help to know that thought has no verbal language. For example, if you wanted to pick up a piece of paper, do you actually think in WORDS, I ... am ... going ... to ... pick ... up ... the ... paper?
Or – do you just do it?
You just do it of course; it is the natural motive of your consciousness, the same consciousness that lives on after so-called death.
Everything in the Spirit World is instant with no need for verbal language, therefore not only do the spirit people have to slow down to our vibrations, they also have to use the spoken word to communicate with us, a procedure which is not a necessity in their world.
The Spirit World communicates through the power of thought.
So - when you suddenly, for no reason at all, think of a deceased loved one, it is likely that the consciousness of that soul has blended in

with your aura attracted by your love, and that is how, in some ways, your loved ones can get closer to you now than they could when they were on the Earth plane.

Always remember that they are only a thought away and like-attracting like plays a big role in the acceptance of unconditional love."

For readers who have little understanding of physical phenomena, below is a brief explanation.

Clairvoyance and clairaudience are subjective methods of communication where only the medium can see, hear or sense the spirit person relaying messages to the recipient. In Physical Mediumship, physical manifestations are objectively produced in a séance room where every sitter in that room can see, hear and be physically touched by any spirit person walking out to greet the circle members.

Ectoplasm, upon which the phenomena depend, is part of the medium's vital energy and is extracted from any opening in the physical body as well as the solar plexus. In nature it is neither physical nor spiritual and lies between the two states of existence – unique to neither but common to both. It can be converted from the invisible state to the visible state as it passes through its different stages of manifestation. It is also light sensitive and severe injury can be caused by the sudden introduction of unexpected light. The spirit people use the ectoplasm to show themselves and we are able to see such materialisations in a dim red light used only with the consent of the spirit team.

Returning to Bob and Ena, Ena's first husband Ronald Hill was killed in action during the Second World War and it was at a Helen Duncan[3] séance that he materialised and stepped out of the cabinet to give Bob and Ena his blessing on their marriage. There is much more about this wonderful spirit connection which can be read in Bob and Ena's book entitled, *'Of Love between Two Worlds'.*

------- 000 -------

_____

3, Helen Duncan was an outstanding physical medium in her day, someone every spiritualist around the 1930s -40s would have been eager to sit with. Through Helen's mediumship, so called deceased loved ones and victims of the Second World War would materialise and walk out of the cabinet to directly converse with their loved ones left on the Earth plane.

Recommended books/DVD relating to this chapter

'Of Love between Two Worlds' by Georgina & Robert Brake (ISBN 9781908421012) can be purchased from Saturday Night Press Publications (www.snppbooks.com). This true story of Bob and Ena's life on Earth along with various poems is an inspiration to us all.

'On the Edge of the Etheric' by Arthur Findlay' (ISBN 9781585093403). A publication every investigator/researcher should have on the bookshelf. The first of many titles involving Findlay's work explaining detailed evidence of the afterlife.

'Life after Death – Living Proof' by Tom Harrison (ISBN 9780951453414). Through the mediumship of Tom's mother, Minnie Harrison, more than 1,500 ectoplasmic materialised Spirit people were witnessed. Read more about this unique circle, the countless evidences and a plethora of phenomena (including photographs of materialised spirit forms) as Tom explains all.

'Visitors from the Other Side, DVD' (can be purchased from Saturday Night Press Publications, (www.snppbooks.com). This makes a change from reading as you can watch and listen to an hour long recording of Tom explaining interesting facts about his mother's (Minnie Harrison's) mediumship.

*'The Two Worlds of Helen Duncan '*by Gena Brealey (H.D.'s daughter) & Kay Hunter (ISBN 9780955705038) Bob and Ena often talked about Helen Duncan and if you wish to know more about her personal life as a physical medium, this book is well worth reading.

'The Sliver Birch book of Questions & Answers' by Stan A. Ballard and Roger Green (ISBN 9780853841005) and for many more other titles - see Spiritual Truth Foundation at www.spiritualtruthfoundation.org.

This 240-page record of straight forward spiritual answers to many questions certainly helped me in my research, an excellent encyclopaedia to have on your bookshelf.

'Jesus Teacher and Healer' by White Eagle (The White Eagle Publishing Trust) (ISBN 9780854871223) and see https://white-eagle-store.org.uk/ After studying the bible, (as mentioned in Chapter 3), this is the book that offered answers to some of my questions leading me to a greater understanding of what could have possibly happened in the biblical days, (See Summary on Chapter 13).

Chapter Eleven

The Séance

Having read about Stewart Alexander in the *Noah's Ark Newsletters*, I was to find out more about his guest séances.

Bob and Ena had been to one at Rotherham on 19th July 1995 and told me how Walter (one of Stewart's main spirit controllers) spoke to all the sitters through Stewart in trance. Below is an excerpt of Ena's report from their book, '*Of Love between Two Worlds*'.

> "To my utter surprise, I heard Walter Stinson say, "I understand there is a Mrs Brake here. Will Mrs Brake please leave her seat and come and sit beside me?" A red light was put on and a way was made for me to do as requested.
>
> Walter said, 'I've a young man here who says he is your husband. He wishes me to give you his love and says you were only married a short time when he lost his life. Is that right?" I told him it was. Walter then said, "This young man tells me you have married again and that your husband is here. He gives him his love and would like to thank him for all he has done for you, that they knew one another and were friends.'
>
> By this time I could feel a hand caressing my arm. Walter said, 'That is not my, nor the medium's hand.' I could feel Stewart's hand still tied to the chair. I realised this was different. I could feel a materialised warm human-like arm and hand, it was a wonderful experience. ..."

As mentioned in the previous chapter, Ena's first husband Ronald Hill was killed in the Second World War just a few weeks after they were married and for her to feel his materialised arm and hand fascinated me, but I did not have the courage to sit in a séance. In fact I was frightened, still frightened of becoming possessed, and the thought of bringing home some kind of unwanted spirit somewhat preyed on my mind. I so longed to experience such physical phenomena, but it was fear that held me back.

In January 1999, an Ark Newsletter announced that Stewart Alexander was accommodating guest sitters in his Thursday evening physical circle. I toyed with the idea of going, but hovered around this thought for some time like a non-swimmer would linger at the edge of the pool trying to build up courage to take the plunge. Finally, I did it. I contacted Ray Lister, Stewart's home circle leader.

I told him I was deaf and wondered how I would be able to cope in an inky black darkroom knowing that there would be no chance of lip-reading. However, Ray assured me that there was nothing to worry about and confirmed I would be sitting next to him so that he could interpret anything important I might not hear.

The 8th of July 1999 was the earliest date he could fit me in and on that day, I entered into the séance room understandably wondering what I was going to experience.

After settling down in the inky black dark room and listening to soft music, it was not long before White Feather (Stewart's main spirit guide) spoke in his Native American accent giving the séance his blessing. Then little Christopher (a 6½ year old boy in spirit) took over and chatted to us all, I was absolutely amazed to hear such a different character with a child's voice and it was his job to relax everybody. It certainly worked on me because all my fears just simply faded away as I listened to his cheeky banter and talked to him. Freda Johnson, another of Stewart's main spirit controls came and spoke to us all in a school ma'amish voice before Walter Stinson with his Canadian accent asked for the table to be moved up to the medium's knees.

I was then invited to sit at that same table directly opposite Stewart.

Little did I know then, that I was about to see ectoplasm before my very eyes, and watch it develop into a solid spirit hand.

A light underneath the glass table top, which was covered with a red cloth, was switched on and I can remember looking at this red glowing oval with great anticipation.

Here is the transcript of what happened:

Walter. You folks who are sitting a long way from the table, if you wish to stand, you may.
Man's Voice. OK. thank you Walter.
W. Katie Ma'am.

Ray. (speaking to the sitters) Just so you can see what is going on, that's all.

W. All you folks here, I tell you what I hope to be able to do.

R. OK Walter.

Katie. Thank you.

W. In a moment I shall produce the energy you have heard referred to as ectoplasm. This I hope to be able to show upon the table-top and from that energy I hope to be able to create, to mould, my own hand folks, but you must tell me if I am meeting with success, for I depend and rely upon you. OK, OK. Raymondo, may we have the music very quietly.

R. Yes

Music plays and Circle hums along with it.

June. Can you see something coming across the table? Can you Katie?

R. Something moving, yes.

(Special note: I was so amazed at what I was seeing, I was absolutely speechless).

J. Something coming across the table-top.

R. It's just sort of spreading. Some of it is spreading; some of it is see-through isn't it?

Others. Yeah, yeah there it is.

R. There's like fingers coming out of it 1, 2, 3, 4. I can see 4, well done friends.

K. Fantastic!

R. You can see where it is transparent in places. Well done, Walter.

J. Well done, Walter. That was successful Walter.

W. OK, OK. You could see?

All. Yes.

W. Then Katie ma'am you must do something for me. Can you hear my voice ma'am.

R. Katie can you hear him.

K. Yes I can.

W. Ma'am, I would like you to place your right hand upon the table with your palm downwards. That is fine ma'am. I ask you to keep your hand perfectly still. Hmm?

K. Right.

Katie places her right hand upon the table.

W. *I want you to tell the folks exactly what you can feel. Hmm?*

K. *Yes.*

R. *What you can see, what you can feel.*

K. *Right.*

J. *Just keep your hand perfectly still Katie.*

R. *What it is like - warm, cold, hot anything and everything about it, just keep your hand perfectly still.*

K. *Yes.*

R. *Now there's the lump, shall we say, coming forward, onto the table, reaching towards Katie's hand.*

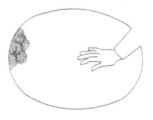

A lump of ectoplasm comes forward onto the table.

K. *It's nearly there but not quite.*

R. *But the hand hasn't formed yet.*

K. *But the hand is coming.*

R. *The hand is forming, can you see it now it's forming. Can you see the fingers now? The fingers are coming towards Katie's hand. (Katie quietly confirms each statement with a 'yes'.)*

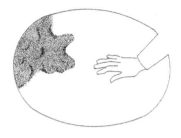

The hand is coming.

J. Keep it down now.

Some of the ectoplasm is transparent as it stretches between the fingers.

K. Yes! Oh I can touch it. Oh! I can. Oh! It's like a real hand.

R. Are they touching you?

J. It's a real hand! It's a real hand!

K. Oh! It's warm, it is warm!

R. Yes. Well that is what they do ... they come back as they are.

K. Oh! It's lovely!

R. Are they touching your hand now? That's good, Walter.

(June chips in 'yes he is').

K. Yes, yes!

There is now a solid hand, touching and stroking Katie's hand.

R. That's wonderful that, Walter. Touching your fingers, still touching your fingers? Is it going back now?

J & K. Yes. It is going back.

The hand returns to being an ectoplasmic blob as it moves back to the medium.

R. It is going back towards the medium. Well done, friends that was ...

J. Well done Walter.

K. That was an experience!

R. That was wonderful, Katie.

W. Ma'am, I hope that it will be an experience that you will never forget.

K. I certainly won't!

W. Of course it is warm and of course it is real, for it is my hand ma'am!

R. Yes, that's right Walter.

W. OK, OK. Ma'am I ask if you would remove your hand and return to your seat.

K. Thank you.

It was definitely not one of Stewart's hands because they were both tied to the chair arms with cable ties and the only way to release him was to cut the ties with a pair of pliers at the end of the séance. I felt quite privileged to have been touched by Walter who passed to spirit in 1911, (almost 90 years ago from the date of this séance held in 1999). I was so excited when I got back to the hotel and so elated to have seen the ectoplasm for real, I just could not get to sleep that night.

Ena had often talked about ectoplasm and I always thought that it was her imagination. What happened that night certainly changed everything and from then on, I no longer simply believed in physical phenomena – I now knew from personal experience that it was genuine.

What Bob and Ena had told me was so true!

Facts, Theories and Anomalies relating to this Chapter.

Subject – Spirit Communication and Physical Phenomena.

This was the ultimate turning point for me.

After that extraordinary event, I would visit more of Stewart's guest circles and write reports using my artistic ability to illustrate a variety of different phenomena seen over the next few years and all my drawings can be viewed in my book, *'Touching the Next Horizon'*.

------- 000 -------

Recommended books and recordings relating to this chapter

*'**Touching the Next Horizon**'* by Katie Halliwell (ISBN 9781908421470) Details various séances with the Stewart Alexander Circle along with 41 recording transcripts.

To listen to White Feather (Track 2); Christopher (Track 3); Freda (Track 4); Walter (Track 5) and Walter materialising his own etheric hand (Track 7) (Available at the time of printing). Visit www.alexanderproject.bandcamp.com (making sure you are on the audio tab and selecting any of the above tracks.)

*'**An Extraordinary Journey**'. The memoirs of a Physical Medium* by Stewart Alexander (ISBN 9781786771377). This book detailing how Stewart became one of the greatest physical mediums of recent time is highly recommended and well worth reading.

'Surviving Death: A journalist investigates evidence for an afterlife' by Leslie Kean (ISBN 9780553419610). Leslie Kean has been investigating Stewart's mediumship for several years and has visited many of his séances. The book also includes a chapter written by Stewart himself. An excellent read if you are interested in not only physical phenomena and after death communications but a variety of other subjects such as reincarnation, near death experiences etc.

'Experiences of Physical Phenomena in the 21st Century' by Ann E. Harrison (ISBN9781908421609). Ann Harrison with her husband Tom were members of Stewart's home circle for 5 years and then returned as honorary members for the next 10 years until Tom's passing, after which Tom returned to the circle a number of times. In this book Ann has recorded many of the amazing communications she had in the circle as well as sittings with other reputable mediums.

Chapter Twelve

Death is not the End

Friends and relatives who knew I had attended this séance were very keen to know what had happened, but not all of them were convinced by my testimony. I suppose like the way I had felt when Ena tried to tell me about her experiences with physical phenomena, they too, wondered if my observations could have been a figment of my imagination. To counteract that reaction, a cassette recording of the actual séance confirmed that the other sitters present had indeed witnessed the same phenomena that I experienced.

With that supportive verbal back-up, I could also let them hear the difference between Stewart's own voice and the spirit peoples' voices, therefore verifying separate entities and characters. I then decided to select the best bits out of the recording and document each one with explanatory notes for anyone wishing to know more about my research regarding spirit communication and physical phenomena.

This worked really well and sparked my enthusiasm to continue with more visits to the Stewart Alexander guest séances with the intention of gaining more information for my 'read and listen' guide.

Eventually this simple photocopied book developed into fifty-two pages with an accompanying cassette offering twenty sections of selected recordings. The title for this booklet was *'Experiences of Trance and Physical Mediumship with Associated Phenomena'* - *'Part One'*. Unbeknown to me at the time, this little booklet and cassette was to be the start of a successful trilogy.

After sitting in quite a few of the guest circles, I was invited by Freda (in spirit) to become an honorary member of the home circle.[1]

---

1. The Stewart Alexander home circle differs from the guest circles because the regular circle and honorary members know how to give out energy to the spirit people, thus providing an opportunity for the development of further phenomena. While in a guest circle, new comers are often nervous and apprehensive – thus taking energy from spirit.

It was indeed such a privilege to witness more intense phenomena and my first visit to the home circle took place on 9th April 2002.

Later that same year, I had the opportunity to meet Tom Harrison and his wife Ann who also happened to be by that stage honorary members.[2]

Impressed with my work they were keen to help me turn the budding trilogy into a professional printable publication. Ann also very kindly spent many an hour audio typing the recordings so that transcripts for the deaf and hard of hearing could be included and the companion cassettes were eventually replaced by CDs.[3]

To celebrate the launch of Part One in its professional form, this home circle photograph was taken in August 2003.

From the left: - Tom Harrison, Katie, Stewart and his sister Gaynor, Ray and his wife June, Stewart's brother Mike and Tom's wife Ann.

Being an honorary member of a home circle gave me the opportunity to see, hear and experience phenomena I had never previously witnessed and I found myself writing further reports and

---

2. They had been full members of the home circle for five years through the 90s, before moving to live in Spain in 2000.

3. All published through their company *Saturday Night Press Publications.*

illustrating different manifestations that were clearly visible to the material eye. Those special evenings certainly gave me the ability to broaden my input and determination to complete the trilogy.

A lot was to happen between the years of 1999 and 2011 and the trilogy developed into an informative source of tangible physical phenomena offering excellent evidence of life after 'so called' death.

With the success of these three booklets and the accompanying CDs which provided a window into the séance room for people who may never be able to experience it for themselves, I decided in 2019 that the time had come to condense all three booklets into one volume. This decision was made in cooperation with the current members of the circle. Instead of separate companion CD recordings, these, at the time of going to press, are now available on-line enabling readers to listen to the voices of the spirit team as we heard them within the séance room. This single volume book, titled 'Touching the Next Horizon' was published in 2021 and is also available in digital form. (eg. Kindle etc.)

During the period of writing the original trilogy, February 2001 saw Ena make her transition into the Spirit World and Bob followed her two years later in May 2003.

My stepmum Myra passed to spirit in January 2007.

Sadly, 2009 turned out to be a tragic year when Stewart's sister Gaynor was a victim of a fatal road accident in February. She was one of the main stalwarts of the home circle and always sat at Stewart's left hand side.

Tom Harrison also passed to spirit in October 2010.

But death is not the end. We have been told that Gaynor and Tom are now part of a special circle in the Spirit World continuing with their work encouraging our circle on Earth to help spread the word about life after death.

Facts, Theories and Anomalies relating to this Chapter.

Subject – Spirit Returns.

The 'so-called' deceased people mentioned above have all taken part in after death communications and as a taster I thought you might like to read about Ena, Gaynor and Tom in the appendices at the end of this book.

Ena came to tell us what a lovely time she was having in the Spirit World. Appendix 1

Gaynor often communicated with the circle and at one point materialised her hand stretching out to touch her daughter Lindsey as illustrated below.

Stewart. in trance, uses both hands to cup Lindsey's right hand.

He then moves his left hand over the top of Lindsey's hand and keeps it there.

Gaynor's hand materialises on the top of Stewart's left arm and hand and reaches out to Lindsey.

And for something completely different from physical mediumship, you might like to read about Annette Childs, Ph.D., a lady in America, a complete stranger who came into contact with Stewart and linked up with Gaynor in spirit. This remarkable true story is detailed in Appendix 2.

When Bob showed me the video of Tom Harrison back in the late 1990s, never in my wildest dreams did I think I would be meeting and working with such a wonderful man. Tom's determination to carry on with his assignment of spreading the word about life after death continued on, even after his own transition in October 2010 and three weeks later he made his first return to the circle, on 16th November, see Appendix 3.

So – Death is certainly not the end.

------- 000 -------

Recommended books relating to this chapter

'Touching the Next Horizon' by Katie Halliwell (ISBN 9781908421470) Find out more about Stewart's physical mediumship and how the spirit people communicate.

'Harrison Connections – Tom Harrison's 'Desire to Communicate.' by Ann Harrison. (ISBN 9781908421111) This is the one to read If you wish to know more details about Tom's many returns after physical death.

'An Extraordinary Journey'. The memoirs of a Physical Medium by Stewart Alexander (ISBN 9781786771377). This book detailing how Stewart became one of the greatest physical mediums of recent time is highly recommended and well worth reading.

'Soul Messengers' (ISBN 9781073099627) by Annette Childs, being a true story detailing how a deceased wife manages to make spirit communication breakthroughs to her sceptic businessman husband and also stays in contact with the author.

Chapter Thirteen

Summary

During my early years, I was a member of a Congregational church, but eventually, I had to stop going to their Sunday school because I was unable to participate with not being able to hear. Having said that, I found it easier to learn more about the Christian teachings at the deaf school and I loved the stories about Jesus.

I would recite my prayers every night in parrot fashion until one day as a teenager I began to question why I was doing this, saying the same old prayer over and over again. After much thought, I began to ask myself questions – What is God? – Where is he? – Where is heaven? That was the time I decided to study the bible in meticulous detail looking for answers to my questions, but I didn't find any.

It was much later in life that one book, *'Jesus, Teacher and Healer'* by the White Eagle Publishing Trust did provide some answers I could relate to and this brought me to the conclusion that Jesus was a teacher of love. From then on, I began to see his parables and miracles in a different light.

Although I class myself as a free spirit and do not belong to any religion, I owe a lot to Christianity and I owe a lot to Spiritualism despite the fact that it took me such a long time to pluck up courage (in 1989) to visit Huddersfield Spiritualist church. At that time I was frightened of Spiritualism and had I not overcome my fear, had I not met Bob and Ena, I would not be where I am now.

As a youngster I heard that male voice speak out of nowhere (as mentioned in chapter 3) and then in later years I had powerful dreams of astral travelling and experiencing some that were precognitive – no wonder I wanted to know what was happening. It was the Yoga class that taught me how to meditate and that was when I started to see flash pictures and what I took to be, spirit lights.

One day when I was meditating back in the eighties, I asked myself another question, "Why are there so many different religions and only one God?"

Then out of the blue, I received my own answer, a thought that somehow made sense.

My thought was that every human being is like a jigsaw piece displaying its own pattern of colours, (just like we all have a colourful aura).

But sometimes we don't quite understand our colourful pattern and to be able to find ourselves, we mix with people of like mind.

Like working out a jigsaw puzzle, one would assemble the pieces of similar colours into selected groups, – just as we gather with people who we feel comfortable with.

On the jigsaw puzzle, the group of green pieces start to link up and suddenly the truth is revealed. The truth is a tree.

The red group does likewise and a field of poppies is discovered.

The blue pieces announce that their truth is a beautiful sky.

The moral of this short story is that as groups of people, we only know a portion of the truth and it is impossible for one school of thought to determine what another school of thought should do. This is probably why to this very day we have so many different religions and organisations on this Earth.

Should you have the ability to rise above this great jigsaw table called Earth, you would then be able to see more of the greater picture. You would see a wonderful scene developing, as opposed to just an individual tree, a field of poppies or a beautiful blue sky.

But being happy in our groups, we still play an important part in helping to build up that picture of love, peace and harmony in our own different ways.

And finally, when the picture is complete, we will become as one united whole.

So it doesn't matter what religion or organisation you choose to join because that is where your heart will want to be at your time of learning.

We are all pupils on this great school called Earth and I can only tell you of my own conclusions based upon my limited level of knowledge. Yours however may be more advanced than mine and you may know far more than I do.

Whatever level we are at, I think it is important to be open about such phenomena and appreciate that not all mysteries will be solved in our life time. Like Jane will probably never find out why she had her time warp experience and Adrian will be left wondering about his mother-in-law, but this does not stop us from investigating further into the enigma of consciousness.

Stepping into Bob and Ena's room and seeing a library of different philosophies, theories, religions and organisations made me realise that my learning was only at the tip of an iceberg.

This is why my recommendation of books is so varied and I hope that this publication will have helped to point you in the right direction towards your chosen path.

Life is a wonderful adventure and I chose the trance and physical phenomena path. My book, '*Touching the Next Horizon*' will tell you much more about my investigation into life after physical death.

Even now, there is still a lot to discover and learn because:

Wherever we walk, there will always be another horizon.
Such is the continuity of life.

May I wish you all the best in your own personal research and I hope that you will find that missing piece in your jigsaw of life.

Katie x

Appendix 1

Georgina Brake (Ena) communicates for the first time.

Home Circle Séance – 15th October 2002. (3 min. 23 seconds).

Excerpt from *'Touching the Next Horizon'*

The recording is available on-line at the time of printing. If you wish to listen to it – visit www.alexanderproject.bandcamp.com and select Track 16.

In this section, you will hear Ena come through in spirit to talk to the members of the home circle for the first time. I was not present at this particular meeting and Ray kindly recorded the message and posted the cassette tape to me. In the recording you will hear Ena saying, "I have met with Medi". The circle members did not have a clue what Ena was talking about. If I had been there, I would have responded directly because I know who 'Medi' is. Many years ago Ena often sat with Mrs MacHattie, a medium who was fondly called 'Medi'. [1]

Happily, Ena is now meeting so many people and having a wonderful time in the spirit world. The recording is very quiet and breathy but worth listening to.

Initials used for those who spoke:
M. = Michael (member of the home circle)
R. = Ray Lister (circle leader)
J. = June Lister (Ray's wife)
Spt Voice and Spt Ena (Georgina Brake in spirit)
G. = Gaynor (member of the home circle)

————

Michael. Come on friend... Yes... We can hear you.
Ray. Come on, friend.

---

1. Read more of her in *'Love Between Two Worlds' (see page 74)*

M. We can hear you, come on.

R. This is good, yes.

M. Well done.

R. This is good, my friend.   (A whispering is heard)

June. So strange – yes.

M. It is isn't it.

R. Is that what they said – so strange.

M. It's very hard to do, isn't it?

Spirit Voice. (whispers) Yes… You… can… hear… me?

J. Yes, sweetheart.

R. We can hear you.

M. You are doing very well.

Gaynor. You are doing very well.

(Breathy sounds can be heard as the spirit tries to speak)

M. That's it, come on.

R. That's it. You're getting stronger.

G. Keep going.

Spt. Voice. I… didn't… quite.. imagine… that … the … day … would … come … when… I … was … communicating… in … this… way…

M. Glad you are.

Spt. Voice. Yes, yes. Can… you… pass… on … my …love …to… Bob.

June. Bob, Yes

Spt. Voice. and … to… my… Katie.

J. Katie? Of course we can.

Spt. Voice. It's Ena.

R. It's Ena.

J. I'll do that, Ena. Bless you, we'll do that.

R. We'll let them know you've been.

M. Well done, Ena.

R. It's nice of you to come, as well.

Spt. Ena. I… have… wanted… to … do… this… for…a …long…time.

R. Oh, you're welcome.

Spt. Ena. Never..thought .. that… I … would… be … able… to… manage… before… this… evening… yes.

J. That's wonderful; you're doing a good job.

Spt. Ena. Give… my… love… to…

J. We certainly will.

Spt. Ena. ... I... have... settled... down... where.... it... is... all... that... we... could... possibly... have ...imagined... Much... much...more.

J. Brilliant

M. That's wonderful.

Spt. Ena. Oh! I ... have... met... so...many... people.

R. You've met so many people?

Spt. Ena. Oh yes! I'm... having... a... wonderful... time.

R. Good. Oh, She's having a wonderful time?

M. That's good.

Spt. Ena. I.. have... met... so... many.... people. 'Medi, yes. I... have... met with...'Medi'.

Gaynor. 'Meeni'?

J. With whom Ena? Who have you met with, Ena?

Spt. Ena. So... many... people. I've... been ...speaking... to...Mrs... Duncan.

G. Mrs Duncan, Excellent

R. Mrs Duncan, that's good!

J. That's wonderful.

Spt. Ena. Yes. I'll... try... again.

J. Oh you must!

G. All right, all right, Ena.

R. You please come again.

J. You must come again.

G. Bye, bye now.

M. Well done! That was very well done.

J. Well done, sweetheart. Thank you, bless you.

Appendix 2

Gaynor Communicates Mentally

An Excerpt from '*Touching the Next Horizon*'

A lady in America by the name of Annette Childs had purchased Part One of my trilogy in January 2009 via the Amazon website. Subsequently she emailed Ray Lister asking if he could send her the accompanying CD. She later obtained a copy of Part Two together with its two CDs. Ray informed Stewart that he had exchanged emails with the lady and Stewart felt strongly that he should make personal contact with her. When he did so, he was to learn that she had a Ph.D. in Psychology, had a private practice working with the dying to assist them in the attainment of spiritual peace, and that she was also a bereavement counsellor. Additionally, she had published important research findings on near death experiences, and since childhood she had possessed a mediumistic faculty although this apparently played a minor role in her professional life. Also, she was the author of two books[1] concerning matters of spiritual communication, and both had won literary awards.

Although Annette Childs had read many books and researched extensively in the field, she had known nothing of physical mediumship until she had come across my work. I also understood that she had known nothing whatsoever about Stewart's personal life. However, not expecting that the two had, by chance, made contact, Stewart sent an email in which he mentioned Gaynor's passing and in return received wonderful words of comfort.

Later, because he understood the great value of communication through a third party, he asked Annette if she would try to link with Gaynor and to let him have any impressions that she might receive. Stewart, as Gaynor's brother, fully appreciated that anything that came through his mediumship would be of limited value for obvious

---

1. '*Halfway Across the River*' – now reprinted as '*Soul Messengers*' (ISBN 9781073099627) Also '*Will You Dance*' (ISBN 9780971890206)

reasons. But any relevant apparent communication coming via a stranger – a stranger in America whom he did not personally know, and who knew absolutely nothing of his personal life – would be so important.

The result was that several days later the lady emailed information that she felt may have been communicated by Gaynor. One episode she mentioned from their childhood remarkably referred to a snake. Annette could not have known about a sickening incident that involved a pet snake and which, although at the time had been very repugnant, nevertheless, over the years, when recollected, had caused the brother and sister great mirth. Stewart told me that when he was a young boy he had persuaded his parents to buy him a pet snake. Unfortunately he was terrified of it and so had kept it in an empty biscuit (cookie) tin with holes in the top through which he fed it maggots. For many weeks he dared not remove the top, and when he finally did so he was to discover that the maggots had made a meal of the snake. Gaynor had been there to witness this and, indeed, they had spoken of it only a few days prior to her untimely passing. Remarkable!

Dr Childs had also given the first letter of a town that she insisted was situated by the sea and which had a great significance to Gaynor. Stewart himself had no knowledge of it, but upon contacting Gaynor's youngest daughter Lindsey, it was confirmed that this piece of information was very relevant indeed to her mother. It was a town on the coast of Cornwall, where, apparently she would have purchased a house if ever she had been so fortunate as to win the national lottery.

The third piece of evidence involved a bouquet of flowers - a full description being given. That morning was Mother's Day here in England and Lindsey had purchased, for her Mum, flowers that perfectly matched the description given by Annette Childs, therefore proving that Gaynor had been very aware of her daughter's gift to her. All of this was marvellous evidence that she had indeed communicated through a perfect stranger in America. The astounding aspect of all of this cannot be underestimated. Indeed, wonderful. Well done Gaynor.

Gaynor has since spoken to the circle and to Lindsey several times, through her brother Stewart.

Appendix 3

Tom Harrison's first return to the circle

Home Circle Séance – 16th November 2010. (5 min. 02 seconds).

Excerpt from *'Touching the Next Horizon'*

The recording is available at the time of printing. If you wish to listen to it – visit www.alexanderproject.bandcamp.com and select Track 26.

In just over 3 weeks after his passing, Tom came through Stewart's trance to speak to the home circle, with a little difficulty at first. A little thing like death was not going to stop him communicating. So I invite you to listen to Tom's first communication with the circle.

Having introduced himself, Tom had something special to say to Chris Eldon Lee, a regular visitor to the circle. Then Walter (a spirit communicator) addressed the circle.

This is what Chris Eldon Lee wrote to Ann after the sitting:

'As you will almost certainly know by now, Tom made a remarkable entrance at Hull on Tuesday. He chose a select audience, with just the five of us there – Ray, June, Lindsey, Stewart and a very privileged me. Funnily enough my eyes had been drawn to study the wedding photo on Ray's wall in which Tom stands so strong and statuesque. So it didn't come as a complete surprise.

His was the first voice to be heard and he came through almost at once, indistinctly at first calling 'June, June' and then more clearly. He told us off for trying to guess who he was before he'd had chance to introduce himself. But his voice gave him away. It sounded just like Tom.* It could not possibly have been anyone else. ...

I must say that for the very first time in circle, the hairs on the back of my neck stood up and tingled and tingled whilst he was present. It was a very powerful and moving feeling and I was so very glad to be present.'

*As Ann commented later ..."And Chris should know the sound of Tom's voice as he spent many hours listening to it when producing the BBC Radio 4 Broadcast *Christmas Spirits* in 2003."

Tom's first return.
Initials used for those who spoke:
Ch. = Chris Eldon Lee (a regular sitter)
R. = Ray Lister (circle leader)
V. = An unknown spirit voice who later identifies himself as Tom
J. = June Lister (Ray's wife)
L. = Lindsey (member of the home circle)
T. = Tom Harrison (in spirit)
W. = Walter Stinson (main communicator from spirit)

(A very breathy voice is heard trying to come and speak).
Chris. Good Evening.
Ray. Hello, my friend. (breathy sound) Nice to have you with us. Come on, you can do it. (breathing again) You're most welcome here, you know. You're most welcome.
Voice. First.. tryv...tryv... Ohh! (exasperated).
June. Clive, no?
V. No.
J. No-no-no-no.
V. Don'...guess ... Don't ... guess. Ohh (sighing, but it sounds like 'June guess')
J. No. It's difficult, come on.
Ch. Come on, come on, you can do it.
Lindsey. It sounds like don't forget.
V. No, don't guess.
J. I've got to guess.
V. No, no, ...don't guess.
J. Don't guess. We haven't to guess. (laughter).
L. All right, sorry. We won't guess.
J. We've not to guess
R. We'll leave it with you.
J. We'll leave it with you, darling, we've not to guess.

R. *Come on. You're welcome anyway.*

Ch. *We understand.*

V. *I...don't...know...if...I...can...say...just...a...few... words (then a long breath)*

L. *(repeating) You don't know if you can say...?*

V. *A few … words.*

June & Chris. .. *a few words.*

L. *You're doing well though.*

Ch. *We'd love to hear your words.*

J. *We'd like to hear you.*

V. *Me...me (a heavy breath then) Tom.*

J. *Tom?*

L. *(excitedly) Yes, Tom. Is it you?*

J. *Tom, Tom.*

Voice now as Tom. Yes.

L. *Tom, you are doing fantastic!*

J. *Love you to bits, Tom. Come on, Tom.*

Tom. Really … trying... hard.

L. *Oh, you are doing great.*

J. *Oh, Tom, it is wonderful.*

L. *Thank you for coming*

J. *This is wonderful.*

T. *Just thought it's time*

L. *You thought it was time.*

T. *For me to come. Yes, yes.*

R. *It's been too long.*

J. *That's wonderful.*

L. *Oh, Wonderful. Oh, thank you for coming and you've done ever so well.*

R. *You have.*

Ch. *We had a great celebration for you.*

T. *Aye, I know.*

J. *He knows. (laughter from the circle)*

T. *Wonderful, … wonderful.*

L. *Are you enjoying yourself over there?*

T. *Wonderful … wonderful.*

J. *Ahh, that's wonderful, Tom*

T. *Tell… Ann… just had to come…I just had to come.*

J. *You just had to come.*

Ch. *You did indeed …*

L. *Thank you so much*

Ch. *What kept you?*

J. *We love you, Tom.*

T. *If I could have come sooner…*

J. *…you would.*

T. *Yes.*

J. *Yes. If he could have come sooner he would have.*

T. *… Ann my love.*

J. *We will give Ann your love.*

T. *Thank you.*

J. *You're welcome, Tom. We love you to bits, Tom.*

T. *Thank you for being here, Chris … Chris.*

L. *Chris.*

Ch. *Tom, it's wonderful to hear your voice, and don't forget that if it hadn't been for you I wouldn't be here at all.*

L. *Ohh.*

T. *Yes, (speaking much more rapidly now)but what… what is important now, is that you are here and everything I said about it, it is all that and more.*

J. *All that and more.*

L. *Brilliant. (with comments on top of each other from the others too)*

Ch. *Absolutely.*

T. *God bless.*

All. *God bless, Tom. / Love you to bits, Tom. / Thank you.*

J. *He grabbed my hand as he..*

L. *He tried …*

Ch. *Is that the first time that Tom…*

J. *That he's been through here, Yes.*

Ch. *…spoken?*

J. *In here, yes.*

There is a creaking sound and Walter takes over control.

J. Hello, Walter.

Walter. Now, folks, that was a surprise.

L. That was a really nice surprise

J. It was a wonderful surprise.

L. He did fantastically well.

W. Well, let me say that he was most insistent.

J. Ohh, was he?

Ch. Funny you should say that.

L. Give him our love.

W. Of course. He has such a will.

J. He has and always will have.

W. You would expect nothing less.

J. No, no, definitely not.

W. OK, so we thought that the time was opportune, particularly since our friend Chris...

Ch. Hello, Walter.

J. ... was here, yes.

Ch. That's very kind, Thank you.

W. You were able to hear him?

J. Yes, yes we were.

Ch. I was looking at his photograph on the wall downstairs just a few moments ago. (The photo is of Tom giving a Spiritualist blessing at Chris and Hannah's wedding in 2009.)

W. Yes. He is insistent that his wife, Ann, is informed.

J. Ray will tell her, won't you Ray?

R. Yes I will.

J. Ray will let her know.

W. OK, OK.

P.S. Ten months later, Tom materialised at the circle and held Ann's hand. (Detailed accounts of this are in 'Touching the Next Horizon' and 'Harrison Connections'. Recordings are also available at the time of printing. If you wish to listen to them – visit
www.alexanderproject.bandcamp.com and select Tracks 27 & 28.)

Milton Keynes UK
Ingram Content Group UK Ltd.
UKHW021837151223
434457UK00004B/11